{ the silence between words }

MARNIE KANAREK

Copyright © 2013 Marnie Kanarek
All rights reserved.
ISBN: 1475227981
ISBN-13: 978-1475227987

foreward by Wanda Lea Brayton	viii
A Subtle Metaphor for Loneliness	1
when you stop pursuing god	2
Odysseus	3
correspondence	3
ache	4
skin deep	4
and if all else fails, there's always booze	5
nearly	6
ursa minor	6
minuet and stone	7
unconditional	7
the clouds point their toes inwards	8
parallax	9
Fractured Inertia	10
soul barer	11
graceland	12
Not meant for casual consumption	13
egress	15
staggering	15
Stone and Needle	16
sentinel	16
he sleeps	17
theos	17
Find your way back to me	19
Incurable	20
Undoing	20
seeds	22
simultudinem	22
Too Long in Moscow	23
Antimatter	24
Reaper	25
the sting of her absence	26
A pastoral lament	27
Descent	27
Malediction	28

empyrean	29
ultimatum	29
Shipwreck	30
inevitable chaos	31
reason rends me red-cheeked	32
hyperion to a satyr	33
a lonely pressing on the chest	33
karumi	35
The inevitability of crash landing	35
sage	37
anne's addiction	37
Epochs	39
a midcentury morality tale	40
Red Giant	41
Lilium	41
The Cimmerian Twin	43
sturtztrom	44
Toxic Savior	44
a quiet stillness among ravens	45
nestling	46
night sky, shivering	46
requiem	47
la fée verte	47
The Course of Things	48
in the key of mourning	48
hung out to dry	50
il m'a fait du bien	50
a fine, white flying myth	51
canticum et cultrum	53
evanesce	53
nexus	54
Pakiwaitara	54
animus	55
wunderkind	56
buoyancy	57
a conversation	58
Confessional	58
carrion	62

hyper music: variations on a theme	63
thru glass	65
Rant in XX	66
songs that sting sad eyes	67
rise	68
a crucial loss of momentum	69
the longest moment	70
mocking the dawn	71
docere, scire	72
asphyxia	72
blur	73
scattered	74
matchstick millenium	74
dark corners quite unknown	75
dew	75
Cracks	76
windflower	77
i hide in folds of twilight	77
green	78
cadence	79
dark-locked	80
the storm that crashed our picnic	80
i won't remember you	81
a heart caged on canvas	82
night rhapsody	83
antithesis	84
time drifts backwards on deep moon eyes	85
the strangeness of becoming	86
a crescendo of green	86
the rise from acquiescence	87
grasping for spring	88
Pearls	88
Equus Nocturne	89
no proof of love	89
Out of Sync	90
art song	91
disgrace and the night apostle	92
a tree draped in winter snow	93

consummation	94
tend	94
transient	95
the dark within	95
ice and stone	97
petals	97
moonstruck at midnight	98
three sheets to the wind	99
ghost	99
pareidolia	101
Mad Ocean	101
slumber	102
inamorata	103
a moment	103
plucked	104
The Remains of Yesterday	104
infidelité	105
inside the void	106
Red	106
bouquet	107
walking in search of sleep	108
sacrifice	108
dissonance	109
The Mockingbird	110
chiaroscuro	110
your eyes are more than color	111
So Young	111
Two eyes, two lungs, one heart	112
quietus	112
The Promise of Rain	113
Gloom	114
courage	114
haiku 1	114
Fragmented	115
The unmistakable calm of trees	116
Clench	116
The Night Parade	117
Exodus	117

I am the travelling moss	118
Water and Stone	118
Between the Trees	119
Lonely Mountain (with Gray Kanarek)	119
The Art of Crying	121
haiku 2	121
White Feather	122
The long road home	122
My eyes unfurl this moonless night	123
winter	123
When you are far away	124
hospital	124
China Doll	125
Sideways Insane	126
Soldier	127
Night Terrace	127
haiku 3	128
Train Ride	128
A whispered song of summer	129
sated	129
Rebirth	130
silence	130
surrender	132
Bohemian Love Poem	132
Greeting my insomnia with a beer	133
The Place Where Grasses Grew	133
The Gardener	135
This Mad Chase	136
home	136
Chasing the Dragon	137
buttercups	137
inside your words	138
Square Blocks, Round Holes	138
dinosaur bones	140
unease	140
Cloudburst	141
paper hearts, origami cranes	141
Where Nothing Speaks	142

open and close	143
poetry	144
Sunrise	144
The king is in his counting house	145
transposed in sky	145
the night we shattered	146
Blank Pages	146
the girl who holds stars on her tongue	147
Searching Stumbling Upon Sad Eyes	148
blackness	148
Believing in the unbelievable	149
The climb	149
star-crossed	149
paperbark tree	150
burn burn the little prom queen	150
Broken Canvas	151
the crux of it all	151
i dream of the moon;	152
The Start of Things	153
treehouse	153
pretend	154
sugar	154
Burden and Butterflies	155
Phantasm	156
when we were young	157
As I Walk On	157
Arcana	158
Pressing the stars of your eyes	159
i constructed a heart	160
The Walk Home	160
The First Moment	161
connect	161
i wish i knew you	163
artfully, i place the pieces of(your heart)	163
Sparks	164
Old Bones Crack with the Strain of Too Much Hope	165
Pandora	166
Snake	167

Asphalt	168
clipped wings and silk screens	168
A cobbled together emotional jigsaw	170
wind against wing	170
Jupiter	171
Little White Bonnet	172
beautiful	173
paper cranes	174
Zeno's Paradox	174
Alone	175
breakfast	176
Broken Dreams and Candle Wax	176
still waters	177
free dissociation	178
Seams	178
Storm	179
the ladder you built	180
Hello There, Little One	181
Bigger	182
Big Fish Eat Little Fish	182
i feel the chest of the world	184

foreward

Artistic people view the world around with a unique aperture. They sense the penumbra, feel the chiaroscuro, of every object, person, element within their circle. They watch from a slight distance with rose-colored glasses, but when things become too dense, too heavy to bear, they put on their darker shades so their glistening eyes cannot be seen by others. Within their craft, they bare their very souls, so it is necessary to keep some things secret and belonging only to them. It is a safety feature, as well as a mystique, a mythology, this veil that creative people reside behind.

I have always resisted any "definition of style", for a photograph only captures a split-second - a painting, only a moment - a poem, only a portion of a day. Just as a book cannot explain an entire lifetime, we must not assume we know this person so well to say they are this or they are that, for they are still on their own journey of discovering themselves. We should not ever declare a single category or a specific genre to describe their art, for that would mean we have consciously filed them neatly into a single box with a label, to be put away to gather dust on a hidden shelf. Human beings are so much more complex than that - and far more simplistic, too.

Marnie Kanarek's words are paintings, tapestries, sculptures, musical compositions ... each one is original, drawn from a deep well of clarity. Her perspective and use of language is elegant, honest, raw, personal, wise, innocent and evolutionary. Her poems are intricate and graceful, but do not hesitate to suddenly jump into the river with their clothes on, laughing at the absurdity of this human experience, the sheer joy they are submerged in - they are acutely aware of truly being alive, not merely surviving. The following lines, written in September 2013, are an excellent encapsulation of who she was and what she was thinking at this particular instant:

> "curled like pearls
> in a deep, moonless sea --"
>
> — excerpt from the poem "a double bind"

Read her words and allow yourself to be immersed in and nurtured by warm currents of a river without end, a river reaching out for the infinite sea. Pass this book along to your loved ones; let it be a part of the legacy you would wish for them, an understanding of one small corner of their world - and invaluable knowledge of the universe they inhabit for a brief period of time. Perhaps they, too, will learn the lesson of cherishing moments that will not come again.

— Wanda Lea Brayton, author of "The Echo That Remains" (Collected Poems)

A Subtle Metaphor for Loneliness

The winter snarls a sonnet in my ear —
I fear the cold, a poison-tipped refrain
that seethes within my veins this time of year.

Your smile has become a frozen sneer:
a sun succumbed to greying clouds and rain.
The winter snarls a sonnet in my ear.

I walk the roads of sorrow, far and near,
excising all your sins to numb the pain
that seethes within my veins this time of year.

But time does not heal troubles held so dear —
these memories are welded in disdain
as winter snarls a sonnet in my ear.

I cannot bear to shed another tear
for you, the one who left my heart insane;
you seethe within my veins this time of year.

I wait, uneasy, for the sky to clear,
to break your curse upon this dark terrain,
but winter snarls a sonnet in my ear —
it seethes within my veins this time of year.

when you stop pursuing god

your finger
rests softly on my collarbone

innocent, almost

as you wheeze a
vodka-laced breeze
into my ear

    i tremble, as a
        hummingbird might

caught between your
smoke-soaked pillow talk
and lazy sneer

the careless way you play
off my fear

    by fiddling idly with your belt

you stroke my hair
as i purge myself

shot after shot

of ill-consumed hatred
burning its way
      back to the sea

i close my eyes
against endless tile

    and you are there

spreading me
like dandelion seeds
in a field of foxglove

Odysseus

my heart has waited
      for fading sighs
of september

      for autumn leaves to fall

he carries the scent
of clove and tall pine

and i rush like a zephyr
      into weary arms

'i love you's suspended
in the knots of his beard

correspondence

i gaze out the window:

the glass is lined
with the thick grime of fall.
outside, trees huddle their limbs
in an attempt to stave off the frost —

leaves hum
to keep from weeping.

the mailbox sits at the road,
cock-eyed, omniscient,
rust nestling its sharp corners.

    there is no mail today.

the leaves give up their long fight
against the ground.

i cannot bear the sight of it.

i will not let go so easily.

ache

there were days

when moon
shivered
on pale skin

and the ache
of old bones

couldn't keep out the rain

skin deep

your oasis eyes
veil a rotting core

august grasses
trampled
by endless drought...

night grows black
pretty girl,
and the moon wilts
like aging flesh

as we wait in the quiet
of dry sands
for a whisper of water
to baptize your deception

in the inevitability of winter.

and if all else fails, there's always booze

it's time to see through all the shit
wade through lies
and spy like a fly on the wall
the fall of all that is holy

what's wrong with
knowing what you want
it haunts you like a wicked ghost
wrapped around your tongue
keeping in all the secrets
burning you alive from the inside
an insidious facsimile
of what might have been

if only time were a teller of truth
instead of scripts and stories
checked off in moments
superstellar windows
into the souls of the sold
bargaining gin and sin
for a leaf of deceit
pressed between unsteady legs

your eyes can't stay closed anymore
there is no more time for rhyme
or reason
or hope
as the rope grows tighter
with every breath
a woven death circling like hawks
around fragile necks

so stop telling yourself
what you want to hear
and feel the sear of light
as it cracks against your skull
letting you know that you have a voice
and that the night is only forever

for those who choose
to live in the dark

nearly

he reaches through moments

muddled memories
    swept into dusty corners

for a fleeting glimpse
of the lotus-eyed girl

who remains

ursa minor

night glistens with
northern eyes

   stars clustered
in a delicate carriage
of sky

as i foster their
seraphic slumber

the mythology
of each moment
cradled

in cloud and caress

minuet and stone

you are still,
cradled in earth

   while rivers
   sulk lazily
   over ragged rock.

I see you in
falling water,
    stretched effortlessly
    as shadow,

each milk-blue cheek
quiet as rain.

your eyes are crescents,

        waning

   as if you were asleep:
   the son I couldn't keep.

unconditional

i would
rend silence
   with my screams

artlessly
   blinding
  the stars

to keep you safe

the clouds point their toes inwards

there are times
when i feel my bones rattle
with each breath of autumn wind

stargazers undressing petals
to whispered reminders
that spring
is a million miles away
      under our feet

so i tuck another piece of myself
inside this mosaic of scars

trying to catch up with the gallop
of unwritten hearts on a sky
pale as paper

but i cant seem to
    pattern my thoughts
  into words

so instead

i stare into the eyes
of a thousand mirrors
and greet the ghost that hides
inside my skin
    bitter as ink

trying to remember
what it feels like

      to make sense

parallax

focus finds the horizon
among whorls
    of
        leather-bound words

worlds unwinding
with the chronic pursuit

of wisdom

*

  but we breathe song
into ancient oak

triads of trust

carving
    rhyme and rune
into rough bark

with the artistry of spring

Fractured Inertia

curtains swirl like spectres,
    arcane and elusive —

chandeliers chatter,

but i hear nothing
as fog creeps eerily
out of gaping mouths,

    oppressing my senses.

shadows silver
    into silence.

*

in the attic,
an echo of sequins
slinks from an ancient trunk.

she speaks of summers
in shy grass,
    nostalgia tickling
faded cheeks

until dawn sneaks in
through unwashed glass

    and she slides
back down
into mothballs.

*

sand swallows my sandals,
rising in ribbons
    from the sea.

enormous jaws
clamp on weary soles,

and a whirl of polka-dots
clatters into ocean tile.

shark eyes
descend
from the sun.

*

unwritten music
burns my skin,

   scoring dissonance
   and discontent
   into each breath.

the dead gather whispers
wrung around
    pale throats:

a noose of linens
   to blind my flesh awake.

soul barer

we steal secrets from
    wine-dark branches,

flesh plucked by fingers
stained with twilight,

slick with sin.

  as hungry mouths
grow sick
on sweet nectar,

she quietly
   slips from her skin.

graceland

shadows of sex
mingle with booze
and whispers of cheap satin

an insignificant distraction
from the bitter grasp
of metallic promises

barely clinging to life
    on a too pale finger

Not meant for casual consumption

I woke up this morning in a blaze of uncertainty,
just like every other day this week,
this month,
this year.
The stresses of life make the pitter-patter of rain
sing like blame and shame and a thousand
guns barking against my window,
like hell hounds have been loosed in my mind,
rabid and hungry for a slice of my endless indecision.

I rack my brain for a bit of peace, a sense of calm,
but all I end up with is a little less luck,
and a clusterfuck of emotion, as the looming lights of
some unknown stage blind my eyes to anything
that might take me away from what's hiding underneath.

Maybe it's not a bad thing,
maybe we shouldn't try to play pretend with our lives,
consorting with the churlish monster that's filled
to the brim with greed and selfish needs,
undermining our freedom and honesty and passion,
sticking filthy, rancid claws into thrice-wounded flesh
to expose a heart half-lost, half-found,
but still fumbling in the darkness for a whisper of certainty:
for one microscopic glint of happiness
amid years of uncharted tears and debris.

There is a voice that hides there, you know,
inside the muck and the waste.
Just a small voice, ruminating like the lorax
in tree stumps, going on about trees and thneeds
but never actually getting a damn thing done.
The lorax was a coward, you know.
I'm sorry but it's true.
If he would have just once stood his ground and
punched that old once-ler right in his ugly green face,
maybe things would have turned out differently for him.

I guess what I'm trying to say is that talking doesn't work
unless there is intention behind those yammering jaws.
And since all I do is talk,
and think so much that my brain must resemble the aftermath
of an apocalyptic zombie attack,
I'm stuck sitting here in limbo,
talking to myself,
talking to you,
going on and on to anyone who will listen
to the garbled ocean of notes I sing
about life and choice and time,
but am utterly paralyzed when it comes
to actually getting up and doing something about it.

Maybe it's common,
this violent stranglehold on our actions;
the ability to move forward has been hidden deep down for ages,
where Adam and Eve first tucked it away
under that tree, under their fig leaves,
where even God couldn't find it.

But here's the funny thing:
that little voice, long concealed beneath
years of self-deprecation and doubt,
suddenly won't shut up.
It wants to come out and shout
and remind of all the things we lose
when we're trying to plan out every breath so carefully
that we forget how to simply exhale.

That voice (not so little anymore)
keeps going on and on about being a person

of consequence, of conscience and substance
without the frills of arrogance adorning every step we take
on the road back to who we were, and who we are,
telling us to drag our sorry asses
down infinitely twisted paths,
falling like the transatlantic-drawl
(not quite here and not quite there)
toward a blank meadow dotted with bits of horizon,
just waiting for the chance to be put back together,
finally home, pressed against the sky.

So it's funny that I'm here, giving advice, and still talking,
telling you to do all the things I am terrified to do —
afraid to leap from the safety of sleep,
from the comfort of too-tight skin
into the vast unknowns of tomorrow.
It might even seem hypocritical,
defending the 'do as I do' quotes,
blathering on about how my chance has passed,
but maybe there is still time for you.

Well, fuck that.

Our chance is now, it has always been now,
and will keep on being now,
until we finally start listening
to the melody plucked on our heartstrings
by the little man with the lorax voice
who has been screaming at us
to move, to act,
to do something to change our course:
to be stronger, and smarter, and start truly believing
that tomorrow can be better.

Because eventually, (and this is the truth)
if I just stay where I am right now,
I think I will be covered in so much mindless pollution
that the sky won't want my sad horizon back,
and all that will be left out there among the black
is a headache,
a tear-stained copy of Dr. Seuss,
and one hell of a lot of regret.

egress

death rises
from his crumpled mouth:
patterns that strain to escape
through the small
    hospital window.

his chest rattles —
a bottle-caught wind
desperately seeking the sea
before it slips away
into darkness.

a flurry of white coats
ebbs into ghosty stillness.
outside,
a paper-gray sky
    remembers to rain.

staggering

trees turn to ash
and my eyes burn
like summer grass
since your fickle tongue
flicked lies toward the sky
and made me feel small

    now i'm more alone
    than i have ever been

    hollow as bone
    in this home
    carved from deceit

Stone and Needle

It's too late —

the cosmic serpent
   hides in shadows,
smoke-curled
beneath her breast

   plucking dead flowers
   from a century of sleep.

Mawu-Lisa kisses skin
stained scarlet
with tears of poppy

enslaved by
rune and thorn.

Nirvana
   still clings
to her lips.

sentinel

the sharp curve
of your jaw
   breeches
a thousand ivied walls
built by years of pity

to swallow me whole

he sleeps

and a blush of sun
runs over river rocks,
fantailed by
   shivers of song.

honeyed dreams unfurl
as night purls
   like an old violin —

 a feline grin
pressed
between pages of sky.

his breath is
feathered footfalls,

heart-flutters
   that capture the quiet
wisdom of rain

held within closed eyes.

theos

he loved to watch
when the feasting began

lovers strewn like grapes
over mad fields
      of epiphany

lost in lust and wine

*

she rode into the
deep thrum of trees

wild and pure

as the moon
     bore down

hungry for the hunt

*

a shield
held across his heart
cannot keep out shame

battle wears him
like a scar

*

from foam and flesh
she rose

wreathed in water

each droplet clinging
to the delicate curve
of her breasts

*

it took one spear to
pierce through darkness

one thrust of his light
and oceans crept apart

revealing dawn

*

she stood
beside him always

a bitter victim

quietly
painting scorn
     across the sky

Find your way back to me

when the wind coos quietly
through my hair
I hear your voice
weaving words half-uttered in bed
mostly-asleep mutterings
muddled deep in dream and ivory linen

my eyes close
and the scent of cool water
too-warm skin
skims my nose

the phantom brush of a limb
the odd echo of an opening door
taunts me
hovers and haunts empty corners
gathering dust
in the eaves of anticipation

with bated breath
i place my heart in trust
and wrap your letters
among the rustle of leaves

let spring touch sweetly
against my skin, slick with dew
and a few lingering kisses

that refuse to wash away with the rain

Incurable

To my heart,

I have memorized you,
every crease and corner,
as dark moves in
slowly, unendingly.

The world collapses around me,
but my eyes
(what is left of them)
are focused only on you —

so as shadow swallows
what remains of our sky,
you are the moon, flickering

in my endless night.

Don't leave,
your Tiresias

Undoing

We think that everything is fine:

pink ribbon-wrapped, shiny bows
tangled inside years of neglect
and abuse and misuse,
and the truth is
no one really gets what it's like
to feel another person's pain.
No,
the edges crumble
like powdered lines of sky
that were snorted off a china saucer
when Grandma wasn't home,
and all we can see from the outside
is the way the light catches

on a glass of sweet tea,
and which sofa the cat liked best
because there's so much fucking fur on it.

It's impossible to be within the walls
when we are chained to our own fears,
barred from the scars etched
inside the minds of little girls
with far too many troubles to count
on their pretty painted nails;
as we lash ourselves to the corners
of something someone hid
in bedtime stories under stilted rhyme
and knives disguised as Prince Charming.

So we curse the weather,
and blame politicians
for the inevitability of grief
that finds its way into the cold caress
of apathy and indifference,
without ever noticing the hand that
slides under plaid dresses
for just one more glimpse of power
before the clouds come in
to hide the light completely.

And so the cycle continues —

views crossed like eyes
too blurry with tears to hear the screams,
smothered under layers of paint
meant to invite in the men
that destroyed their youth with one touch,

one thrust that tore through trust,
like the clean edge of a blade
sliding through years
of regretting the chance they never had

because they were too small to fight back.

seeds

my hands plunge into soft earth
to gently lay your wrinkled heads
on dark, damp ground.

i know your hunger

for light
for dry, warm air
and the feel of rain on new skin.

i, too, am hungry

for warm bread
and the taste of cool water,

like you:
blind, yet yearning.

such simple beasts we are.

simultudinem

january fit neatly
in my hand

shivers of wanting
    encased in ice and flesh
unwilling to surrender
to winter's idle whims

it pulsed quietly

a heady thrum
    fracturing the grey

of sky and snow

Too Long in Moscow

winter rambles on, whispers of unborn grass bite
snow's papyrus skin thumbs smudge newspaper ink
onto a coal-black sky, cloud the color of pitch.

we wait for your end, o cold creeping wings of winter
as you thunder behind boudoir windows fogged up
with the sweet breath of sweat-clung bodies,
desperate to undress the steely frost

like trees that silently shiver on edges of highway
slick with ice, kindled by a lone traffic light.

nobly they stand bathed in color; a contradiction
to the lonely drone sprawled across the trans-siberian,
tire-bruised and marred with cloven feet.

we wait for your end, o winter, within the smooth
curve of diner tile; a respite from darker landscapes,
as winds coil around chimney smoke
eager to wrinkle the leather of empty barstools.

how we wait, hidden in warm wooly corners,
while fireplaces charred brick houses hearth dragons
lick the last dying embers of sun, coating us all

with a thick layer of soot.

Antimatter

lately

i find myself
inside
a blank crest
of sky

thumbing
eyelids closed

in an attempt
to shut out
the n o t h i n g

that shrieks
through my skin

the way winter
breathes flame

and pain

becomes
so achingly familiar

that its removal
is worse

than its sting

Reaper

he is silent oak

leather boots
   lurk against roots
that harvest bereaved soles

for something
 stronger than sun
to nourish them

i watch him circle
freshly-turned earth

   a hawk

rending oaths
once woven in flesh

and i weep
for souls
    bereaved

as he scatters
the scraps

    among stone

the sting of her absence

she counts each lash
that falls from her
    pretty little head

trembling, dry as bone

pleading for a
single moment's breath
to launch her un-uttered wishes

skyward

*

love doesn't wake the
too-pale girl glutted with pills

doesn't take away the guilt
   of our acquiescence

love scars
her every breath
into my flesh

*

i keep the most
peculiar fragments safe

the funny curve of her lip

the flick of a wrist
   as she rolled a new cigarette

as i struggle to remember

the tempo
   of her goodbye

A pastoral lament

The trees remember yesterday:
a song upon the leaves of old.
The trees remember yesterday,
when autumn seared us red and gold
with whispered chords of fading sun —
a song upon the leaves of old.
These memories drip one by one
from hazy clouds. They intertwine
with whispered chords of fading sun
like murmurs of the creeping vine.
The years predict our fate's refrain
from hazy clouds; they intertwine
as branches shed their untold pain,
a shrouded voice from veins of green.
The years predict our fate's refrain
with winter's echoed woe unseen,
a shrouded voice from veins of green.

>   The trees remember yesterday.
>   The trees remember yesterday.

Descent

Emerging dawn reveals the eyes
of night undressing her disguise.
A satin mouth unclenches jaws
and yawns, unfurling pregnant pause.

>   The silence thrums, a flower blooms
>   between the stems of milky plumes,
>   unveiling petals, slick with dew:
>
>   a heart restored by breath's debut.

Malediction

The sky howls,
cupping water
in her wide mouth

as we sink deeper
into the black.

Winter is used to such rain,

when dark spokes of night
crack like autumn leaves

and rumbling moss
remembers
the carved eyes
of naked trees

telling stories
pinched out
of angry cloud.

It's time
we whispered back
to their wicked winds,

reminding
of the silence

that follows the storm.

empyrean

pearls of sweat
cling
like a mosaic
    of memory

as quietus creeps in

a shiver of calm
gliding
from the last gasp
of a weary heart

into the stillness
    of dawn

ultimatum

i've wasted years
waiting
for him to grow

a forever child

tied to the petals
of wilted spring

*

you wove a story
of summer

but we were days
of endless rain

i need to see
the leaves change

Shipwreck

With a quick shiver,
the steady gleam of night
carves a cold crescent
in my breast, a test of
strength that I do not have.

The moon rests in a small nest
beneath my ribcage, now
hollow as the moments
spent furrowed

inside your flaccid embrace —
limbs churning in an effort
to arouse passion
from under a wet tongue of linen
that chafes at dove-skin,

like sun and sand crusted
upon scaled knees.

I can no longer fight the wicked
edge of your words, curving
cruelly to my dusty bones.

I crack under your words,
breathing ocean spume
into my lungs.

You shall know my grave
by the salt fumes.

inevitable chaos

the fear
isn't that the world is madness

caught in the spin of acid-clouds

(they remind of home)

as sins are tucked
behind the ear of a dirty girl
smudged with
cigarette burns and freckles

a roadmap of pain

(follow the dotted lines
        to your own heresy)

the fear
isn't that dying is inevitable

we are all just locked
inside quiet bones

tiptoeing through equations
in our milk-white latticework cage

(waiting)

for the right number of reasons
to arrive

at the end

reason rends me red-cheeked

a maiden
dressed in flesh too frail,
sky-pale
  and unaware

shivers down the path
made by his finger trail
clung with the last petal
of spring.

    he unmolds me,

slippery skin
scaled back with sin —

a willow, bone-dry
and bare
as i absorb pain
through knotted roots,

      limbless and weeping.

i shed virtue like rain.

hyperion to a satyr

as shadows fall upon a summer's breath,
a bitter wind contrives beneath the mist
to wraps its tender furls around the wrist
of fractured songs igniting daylight's death.

the sun is forced behind the deep twilight;
a fading glow that startles breathless stars
into a veil of pale and faceless scars
to victimize our sin in shades of spite.

the fear of carving black into the day
becomes a weapon rending winter's reign;
but night rests cruel upon a throne of pain,
and tortures to the tune of willing prey.

the ruthless darkness fiercely battles on
until the mad horizon bleeds with dawn.

a lonely pressing on the chest

the sun melts like a bruise
into the horizon,
slowly washing out
the bustle of day

as wind tugs
at cypress and elm,
reminding them to sleep.

they lay down leaves
to make a bed
for the wild creatures
that live here.

i am one of them.

we are old friends,
the trees and i;

the quiet finds me

lost
in shades of grey,

just another shadow
etched in the landscape
of the forgotten.

*

the world sleeps,
but i am wide awake
among collapsing stars.

you can't stop the mind
from racing in the dark hours;

it's enough to see him
tucked under your eyelids
like rain,

or a branch
heavy
with first snow —

the weight becomes unbearable,

so i busy myself with silly things:
scrubbing silver,
washing floors,

anything to evade
the memories that haunt
when silence arrives
dressed in mourning.

i draw a curtain
over moon's intrusive stare,
hiding behind a flurry of activity,

knowing he is out there somewhere...
carved like a scar into the night.

karumi

拝啓 敬具 Matsuo

in ink-dark night,
sword gave way to brush
under jade moon

> your footsteps
> smoldered in the smoke
> of machiya fires

now you close the gate
and wait for lightness
in your bashō hut

> the words have gathered:
> spring blossoms whisper
> your coming

どうぞお元気で。

The inevitability of crash landing

Blue sparks blaze
behind my eyes,

    and I cry

as metal snags my senses,
rips my heart to ribbons.

You're still trying to fly
in the wide cold sky,

but the land
keeps coming up to greet us
like an old friend with gun in hand,

and I wish
I didn't know this story's ending,
but life just seems to keep on
causing catastrophe
from relationships,
    severed and scarred.

Flames grow higher
and I become more aware of the smoke
that blurs the horizon,
as wiser shadows curl to my bones —

    they speak of rebuilding
    from the ashes of infidelity,

but I can't find my way out
of this wreckage,

    constantly checking compasses
that spin a dizzy dance of destruction
    among the carnage.

So we're stuck here,
dying on an oxygen high:

a one-way trip
to
hell...

"There's only one bullet in the black box,
pilot...

    It has your name on it."

sage

it beats

nestled
  among
cloud paper

(a secret)

hidden
  within
crypt of tree

every twitch
  of autumn leaf
echoes
with timeworn
      whimsy

gathering wisdom

in thimblefuls
of
rain

anne's addiction

I.

oh you,
how the back and forth madness
wrenches sunlight from your hair

cold skin, too tight against your bones

the moon reflects your eyes
two marble eggs, milk white
and glutted with poison

it cries out like a nightmare
hidden under layers of vodka and dust

II.

you cut away your chaotic flesh
like a greasy tumor
revealing a skeleton of glittering stone

oh, how they must have loved you
strolling in with your fur and slick tongue
singing songs of sex and suicide

your easy consummation with the dead
was pressed in ink long before
you took your place among them

III.

there is no more screaming now

no more wounds laced up
with yarn and psychotherapy

the windows are closed
and the white floors of hysteria
have been scrubbed clean

now, only memories remain
tucked up under the skirts
of a stolen childhood

pressed into the bosom of your words

like the darkness
you once called home

Epochs

a corset haunts the waist
of a silly young girl
who thinks
star-flung thoughts
and tosses songs
onto an ocean
of clear, clean blue

possibility clings
to her dimples

an empty womb
goes unnoticed

until it doesn't

ten fingers, ten toes
run across this maze

constantly changing

jigsaw puzzles dance
(in her mind, on the floor)
and a little boy laughs

filling the silence
she never knew was there

until she did

a chaos of curls
frames his face
(her eyes)

and still he laughs
puzzling out answers
that need to be sung

he walks unmarked paths
weeding mad hedges

of wisdom
that grow wild in his mind

he tries to be happy
without her

never truly knowing
how much
she loved him

until he does

a midcentury morality tale

a piece of mind is left behind,
when eyes as cold as coin imbue
a bitter wind with words unkind
to bruise the truth that blooms in you.

the moon reveals your absent gaze
as cadences of blue haiku:
a silent sky on rhyme-worn days
can bruise the truth that blooms in you.

but winter plucked from wrinkled skin
unfurls its breathless crest into
the empty earth of sorrow's twin,
to bruise the truth that blooms in you.

as draft and darkness snuff our flame,
a shadow stained with frozen dew
betrays the scar of ceaseless blame
to bruise the truth that blooms in you.

Red Giant

we laced together
like sand and sea

bodies blurring
against
   hushed horizon

until light
seared our skin

     and we shattered

each bound breath
gasping into flesh

*

you swallowed the sun
that day

leaving behind
nothing
   but a shadow's blush

to illuminate our parting

Lilium

I wait alone in darkness

watered

by a sky I cannot see
   an eye I cannot touch

as voices press down

earth endlessly bruised
by yearly reminders
of old memories

I grow where death lies

*

I am rooted
    born out of eternal sleep

stone makes a cold bed
for one so young

I grow where death lies

*

yearning for warmth

I stretch tender limbs
through mud and moss

time is a veil
    and I do not know green

I grow where death lies

*

they come to desecrate me

plucking the skin
from my bones

as the sun casts a shadow
    over the nameless hundreds
who remain

an epitaph to those
who came before

I grow where death lies

The Cimmerian Twin

the night was cruel
when you hacked yourself
away from me, skin too thin:
a lump of butter, melting on the rack.
teeth yellow, an utter waste of a grin.

now i waste moments, dead in the flame,
like a moth, drawn to sticky light.
i taste pain, the hot searing blame
over eyelids sewn shut:
what a sight.

the moon sneers with pitted eyes,
and i know she seeks me, too:
a shrew, a sister
who could feed you lies
in shrouded skies.
she waits, blue
and pale as water.

> my sins are never as strong
> as the scent of gin
> or a long time spent
> with an old poison.

they laugh from a tin can,
they see what you do not see.

the way we shed blood
made this shadow of a woman,
now free of your mad grip:
an endless flood
from a wellspring of sorrow.

my heart is now dry.
there is no slaking tomorrow.

soon enough,
we will remember how to die.

sturzstrom

unfettered truths
ravel to dust
as clouds of earth
consume us

all that's left
is a glimmer
of rockfall eyes

collapsing
under the weight
of expectation

as we struggle
to extricate ourselves
from the rubble

Toxic Savior

o wicked
wondrous mouth

that smacks with lips
as sharp as nails
over plasticine hearts
that beat backwards

and sucks the stain
from within

half-dead truths
spread like flame
over serpentile tongue

hostile
and bitter as turpentine

and just as deadly
when drunk
straight from the source

*

there's no more time
for newspaper murders

the lies
keep multiplying

like the ghosts in the hall
that stare down
their own glossy throats

bird-pecking away
at the last bits of shadow
still clinging
to an anorexic dream

wasted
by a sense of self-deprecation
and dread

while outside
    the church bells
scream their last good-byes

to the light

a quiet stillness among ravens

the flowers speak in sonnets

rose-petaled fingertips weaving
into the silences
between each breath

the rain howls
through fog-swept eyes
quietly plucking feathers from
another untold story

the whisper of birds within its pages

nestling

morning spatters
frosted light
across the trees

as you move, fitfully,

a blur of feathers
trembling
against an eyelet
of autumn leaves.

the wind
mocks wings

too small

to hold the quiet
in your bones.

night sky, shivering

moon in rusted black

winks

frosted petals of snow
flickering
between eye and lash

cold cheeks
rest
against the stars

as the scent of winter
slowly melts to morning

requiem

softly, winter rumbles
on wide moon sighs,
night birds haunted by
ghost echoes,
smoldering sky with silence.

flakes of snow catch
on cracked wings, as
rhapsodies of white,

appassionato,

hang from bare branches
under violin's crooked bow:
newly formed fingers
grazing frost-chords,
ripened by wind's
yearning.

graves tremble, as years
hum a hushed aria
over blurred horizons,
shivering in tempo with
the snow.

la fée verte

i curl forsaken fingers
around one more glass of

l'esprit bohème

it laces into
sun-soaked veins

like wild ivy
    wandering

in search of moonlight

The Course of Things

The wind catches in our throats
sticky
  like salted caramel

as sand pricks foot soles

carving a waning moon
into each step

Ocean waves breathe verbs
collapsing, unfolding

blurring blues
awash with adjectives

while birds murmur morning
sleep-eyed, wet tangles of hair
nesting just off the coast

We listen
for the pattern-of-poetry
in common silence

a habit, unaware
like stone crabs

and how they dig
their way back
to the sea

without punctuation

in the key of mourning

it wakes me
  like the sleeping dead

a monarch movement
marching over
flickering eyelids

as i breathe
to the beat of
butterfly arms

(opening and closing
against cold glass)

*

the night
shiver-streaks
across empty walls

shadows wither
in swelling scarlet
suspended
like a stain
   on my skin

too stubborn
to fade away

*

just
another
day

spilled across
a rumpled bed
tossing flares
   of awareness
into the void
as morning oozes
through the cracks

and dreams scatter
like field crows
after gunfire

i mourn their absence
like a phantom limb

hung out to dry

i write
and words drip
like dew,

the sweat of song
falling with every blink
of morning sun.

it burns

as raw, scabbed knees
crawl through
meter and rhyme

and black, black ink,
still wet against the sky.

il m'a fait du bien

all was once
grey and dreary
feckless men gasping bullets
at sleek fur

then he appeared

and sun sang
through wheat

as i was tamed
    by the silence
between visits
from a little boy

whom i could call my own

a fine, white flying myth

i sit alone, a figment
in a world grown wild:

too-big boots,
and a smoking jacket
sewn with ghosts.

his name clings to my fingertips,
untamed by fledgling ink
as i, the bronze-eyed baby,
lose winter from my cheeks:

a fatherless child
with grief-stained hands.

*

i know you, mother.

you who taught me to reach
for the quiet born of flame,
for the prick of a quick blue breath —
never to wake
from the sick fumes of blame.

his death made you somber,
made you ache for your own pyre.

fire called to you, mother,
and you rose, bidden, from the ashes,

to stash yourself inside that hell-box:

a foxglove,
thumbed shut by the sun.

*

he stands there —

our hands touch
carelessly, bound by air
and the promise of sunlight,

sharing in the cry
of low clouds.

mingled skin sighs
as we braid flesh together,
unaware of our own seams:

a wedding ring; a puppet string.

*

i worry away days,
lost in the sting
of white-walled solitude.

a ball gag buckles over my jaw —
the snap of rusted metal,

and electricity chirps
like a thousand jeweled birds
inside my skullcap.

it crackles in my hair,
in the creak of brittle bone.

*

my sanctuary spites
the cool caves of cleverer men,
as i, wasted
on a willow's breath,
tuck pills under my tongue;
down, down
into the deep, black brine.

the night is numbed by silence:
hair wet, eyes late-blue.

wanton and without hope,
i wait for you.

canticum et cultrum

two paths wind and diverge
like veins that twist
inside a heart of black,
dark and hard as glass,
shattering the wide belly of night
with whispers of what could have been.

elusive gods breed both eyes blind.

eastward brings music —
wild mosses and mist,
feathered streaks of sun
brimming with passion and possibility.
westward brings blood and bone,
the mottled marrow of words
furrowing like winter hoar
into a cave of cold calculation.

elusive gods breed both eyes blind.

it threatens naked skies with rain,
a stain on the dry, cracked lips of earth
that smack together
to make two halves whole,
but cannot bridge the divide
between song and scalpel.

elusive gods breed both eyes blind.

evanesce

winter braves
    bare branches
but they can't seem
to catch the snow

    before it melts

nexus

the road winds
with westward intentions

curves the moon to my breast

as we mold night
with sand and stone

the hush of winter
reaches fingertips
across cracked flesh

harmonizing our breath
as the cold settles in

to quietly piece us together

Pakiwaitara

Our land was waiting, aching with mistrust
when gods unfurled their breath into the sea,
a call that pierced the wild eyes of lust
enrobed in skin as black as night's marquee.
The wind went howling back into the dust
and silence rode the waves of what could be;
a thrumming deep inside the womb of earth
intoned the twisted fortune of my birth.

Her splintered spirit vainly tried to cope,
but moon began to swell as darkness surged;
a belly filled with mirrored eyes of hope
did quake like ocean tide as life emerged:
a pair of souls, one mad entangled rope
that broke with dawn as boy and girl diverged.
How sorrow bound with fate to make me strong,
is only the beginning of my song.

animus

I met the brute in wild orchards,
and there were no birds in the branches,
only ripe, swollen apples that I counted,
one by one —
a mantra as you pressed your
thick black hate into me.

We must have looked like lovers,
tangled in grass and sweat;

I remember it well,
that ebon heart beating next to mine,
the stench of your skin, like tar,
impossible to rub off
even after you laced up your boots
and walked away,

leaving me in a cloud of honey flies and pain.

*

I knew you'd be back.

I would be ready
to rip out that bruised and bloody organ,
limp with cowardice,

and claim it in the name
of that bastardized garden of eden
where you split me open and invaded me,

but failed to conquer my soul.

wunderkind

My toddler desperately wants
to explain the intricate details
of multivariable calculus
or ask for a cup of milk,
but can't seem to get the words out,
so instead spends his time
shouting and stomping
on chubby little feet —

an adorable dictator
with a mad crown of curls
and big rosy cheeks,
racing around as if sleep were
only recommended, not required.

He burns brighter than a gamma ray,
and no matter what they say
I refuse to dim that fire
to mold a more complacent child.

Instead, I will suffer every arrow
and every sling
that wild boy of mine throws
(with an arm to rival Babe Ruth)
to watch him unfold like Spring,
eyes full of wonder
at the delicate stroke of a crayon,
at pillows in need of pouncing,
or simply giggling at the absurdity
of words such as 'skunk' or 'god bless you.'

I will never understand
how his mind works,
and I'm not sure I want to —
I'd rather marvel
at this remarkable creature
that shares my face and spirit:

curious, stubborn, and strong,

alive in ways
I didn't know were possible.

until he emerged,
slick with the blush of life,
and changed my story forever.

buoyancy

sometimes
we find our sky unraveling

it's a sad truth

life has a way of dragging us
naked and raw
across sun-baked stone

into the cold and the wet

flailing limbs
that sweep wide ocean
    trying to break the surface

or be utterly devoured

sometimes
you have to lose yourself
in the madness
to find your way back again

but sometimes
driftwood makes a home
in the blue

so even if the shore is out of reach

even if you have
no intention of returning

you will have
something solid
to grasp onto

a conversation

i breathe
and black squiggly lines
jut from my lips

words

trembling with such ferocity
   that they are barely understood
by a bird
perched low on the willows

he responses with alacrity

every tweet accompanied
by a chorus of crickets
strumming stories on blades of grass

ancient wisdom
hidden

   within hiccup and hum

Confessional

[1940, eight years old]

Oh Sylvia,

Daddy died yesterday,
lost himself
piece by piece

a foot, a heart
a foolish tongue

while I put words to paper
and watch ink
spill over my hands
like blood.

I try to remember him

but I can't get past the smell
of rotting flesh

of freshly-turned earth.

Sivvy

*

[1953, twenty-one years old]

Dear Sylvia,

I tucked myself away
like a fetus
inside mother's womb

so dark,
damp and dreary

until they found me,

a goose stuffed full
of poison berries

and kissed my eyes open
with the sting of hot metal

on cold, pale skin.

Your loving
Sylvia

*

[1956, twenty-four years old]

Dearest Sylvia,

We walk the beaches
of Benidorm,
eat fish cleaned
from their bones.

his voice slicks my body
like sweat,

a thousand rumbling stones
glistening
in the Mediterranean sun.

Yours,
Sylvia

*

[1961, twenty-eight years old]

Sivvy,

My insides are black
and I retch out sorrow
in pink ribbons

unable to hold onto the life
that once flickered
like the tail of a cat
in my belly.

I have been uprooted,

where forest grew
is now smoke and ash

a sunken moon
hangs between my ribs;

my waist is too supple.

S

*

[1962, twenty-nine years old]

Sylvia,

The summer is hot
and the hives
hum incessantly.

there are so many of them
I cannot discern but a gold cloud;

wings and legs
and sharp little knives
tucked into their pockets.

They whisper scandal.

Always,
Sylvia

*

[1963, thirty years old]

Dearest Sylvia,

He is knitted to her
like the seam of a dress,
tattered and stained,

his rough edges worn
by the winter in her hair
as I untangle
my wicked mane of words

and slowly
stitch them to paper:

my last correspondence

before swirling fumes
wreath my head like a crown

and call me daughter.

Your loving
Sivvy

carrion

fingers plunge deep
into the cavity
where your heart used to be

cold, unfeeling
a bitter shell of what you were

i try to remember
what you were like before
you gave yourself
to those who would tear you down

rip you apart

but all i see is emptiness,
a husk of flesh that stares with
no regard for anyone or anything

as you let them take you apart
piece by piece

and don't even flinch

it's as if you are unaware
of the vultures eying you,
ready to pluck the meat
from your bones

and i am there among them

just another bird of prey
waiting to absorb
even the tiniest spark of knowledge
kept hidden underneath
damp, wrinkled skin

only to be released
by the cool blade of a scalpel
held in the shaking hand
of one pale,

terrified medical student

hyper music: variations on a theme

~allegro~

you wear summer in your hair
fire trembling
in rain-held eyes

sing me a sonnet
pen me an autumn leaf

*

~leggero~

dizzy little faery
   plucks
courage from tears

and tucks it away
under wings

she never knew she had

*

~adagio~

the poppies
cannot help but stare

spring names itself
in the rhyme
    of your lips

*

~scherzo~

another phone call
just to say hello

love is reading the silence
between words

*

~saltando~

hummingbirds
constantly chatter

    a wild nest of curls

how can such a small thing
make so much noise?

*

~cantabile~

dreams rest on her tongue
but she refuses
to set them free

the moon has grown
weary of waiting

*

~mesto~

we scurry along
    labyrinths of dust

as you rise from loam
casting shadows
    across the sky

you are majestic

    terrifying

...why are you so afraid?

*

~agitato~

you stand there
every day
lost in warm mosaic flesh

(such a narcissist)

*

~malinconico~

i rain poetry
    moonlight
  over dark water

hoping my words
find stillness

before they scatter

*

~a tempo~

meaning

lost within the petals
of another
obscure metaphor

where is the music?

thru glass

morning
  streams in
like overgrown
thought-traffic

little black bugs
that crawl
across
  crumbles of sun

ripe
  caffeinated eyes

blink me to waking

Rant in XX

don't think you can own me
with expensive jewels

selling your soul
for an ounce of dignity
all wrapped up in a pretty silk bow

you are as artificial
as that heart of yours
throbbing inside a steel drum

rat a tat tat
and the chains that bind
keep clanking

you say you love me
but all I hear is white noise
and the steady thrum of hoofbeats
echoing against cold metal
as you continue to decay
rotting away
under diamond bracelets and rings

I've seen it all before
I know this game

how you treat women like kittens
distracted by a shiny bauble
purring and pawing at your mottled skin
secretly hoping
you'll drop dead on wedding night

before the prenup is signed
before the very thought of intercourse
makes them heave out their dark intentions
onto the thick white carpet
of the ritz-carlton

I am not fooled by flattery
by piles of money
suitcases of money
checkbooks

and platinum credit cards

no

I refuse to be debased
by your lack of compassion
by your so-called superiority
your insinuating gifts
that cheapen the flesh
clinging to my bones

I do not need adornment
I will not be bribed

I refuse to settle for gold
when the moon above
shines so damn bright and beautiful

reminding me
that I am stronger than they think

that my heart is worth more
than mere trinkets

that I cannot be bought

songs that sting sad eyes

she sings
   ten thousand psalms of longing
to a wandering sea

two hands weaving water
through moon and rust

as night remembers his name
in driftwood
     heavy with salt

rise

rain everlasting

among hidden light
waits sunrise

palms cold within summer
hold songs whispered

night as long silence

green grass eyes
over hazy moon

moon hazy over eyes

grass-green silence
long as night

whispered songs
hold summer
within cold palms

sunrise waits

light hidden
among
everlasting rain

a crucial loss of momentum

electricity
rides waves of memory
like quicksilver

snaking highways that branch
across unbridled emotions

only to catch breath
between the winding roads
of intention
   etched across a restless mind

*

it's all about losing control

a face masked by years of battle
raging inside
this small, dark space
as shaking feet
   slowly shuffle forward

missing something
you never knew you had

until it was gone

the longest moment

red petals shock the grey
of hard, bleak stone
like the first flush of winter
on young cheeks

(you always gave your jacket
at the faintest shiver,
    in the bitterest cold)

the grass is frowning
under my feet
  a weak green, as if
night came and sucked the
vitality out of each blade

(you saw meaning
  in the whisper of trees)

maybe things
aren't meant to grow here

maybe it's better that way

(on that day,
    you held my gaze
and i memorized our love
in the longest moment
i prayed would never end)

without you
the sky is too damn blue

mocking the dawn

i sag from the weight
of a weary world

skin taut
around pink cheeks
wrinkled from stale air
and smoke
    cut off from my sisters
like a diseased limb

every fiber
    sickly green
and soft as the earth
i once called home

the sky calls
through thick glass
whispering courage
      just out of reach

as this electric hum
of florescent sun
heralds my death

a mockery of dawn
that draws nothing

      but moths and dust

docere, scire

i want to heal torn flesh
mend cracks in lightning
     in off-beat
         rhythms
   of heart

i want to wake
the sleeping child
from her canopy of white

remove the demons
who hold on so tightly
to ravaged minds

    twisting vines
  inside a maze
     of wasted words

i want to melt inside your veins
and quench the thirst of
a sickly-sweet mouth

capture sadness in a jar

and disappear it to the
     deepest fold of night

asphyxia

the moon gasps

as my lungs grip night
like well water

each breath
slowly collapsing

     into darkness

blur

you chase the sun
the way wind chases its tail

while i run
for the feel of breathlessness

turn the screw a little deeper
inside my soul
twist it 'round until it whispers
soft ghost chords

and i wink at the moon
as my traveling boots
sink into darkness

*

my fingers played winter
the day the snow melted
under our feet

but you'll never get back there

no matter how hard you clench
your eyes shut
or how many times
you click your pretty red shoes

i just keep spreading my wings
against a storm of stars

blurring the lines between seasons

until summer sneaks up
behind you

golden hoofbeats
echoing
in the wind

scattered

this mad cascade of words
keeps me awake at night
like tiny birds, or fish scales
glinting just out of reach

and the more i try to hold onto them
the more they slip away

so tonight

instead of getting lost in a labyrinth
of my own futile artlessness

i will open my bedroom window
fill my mind with stars
    and creep across the sky

matchstick millennium

rockets burst inside your eyes
like the sun, a clenched fist
and there are too many coins
scattered along this tired street to
follow you home

i'm fading in the curve of your jeans

a strung-out wind, whiteness
wailing for just one more kiss
to smack color back into
my haggard soul

but your breath flickers
like sandpaper inside an endless rain
and try as i might
to grab hold of your galoshes

you are always a thousand candles away

dark corners quite unknown

the sky was under our feet
and we built castles in the
cracks and watermarks from days
of endless rain.

i traced the wind in your hair
as night slowly melted over bottles
of half-smudged memories
scattered across the lawn,

moments filled with nothing but breath
bluer than bathwater —
a million droplets ebbing
with the steady whirl of earth
beneath our heads.

you held my gaze,

whispering the same song
i heard against my mother's breast

before her darkness knew my name,

stripping away innocence
in sheets of blood-tinged cotton
to make room for another glass

clamped between cold hands.

dew

you slick
back the hours
with warm hands

mouth curved
against
the green of summer

Cracks

The winter plucks strings of a mad violin;
I'm losing myself in the cracks of my skin,
a willow's last shiver reflected in eyes
consumed by a darkly-struck soul full of lies.
The crinoline demon of summer forewarns
a last glance of roses unfurling their thorns.
I lock up my nightmares inside of my head
but the past keeps whispering sins in my bed;
no matter how hard I pretend not to care
this terror bleeds rivers my heart can't repair.
The winter plucks strings of a mad violin;
I'm losing myself in the cracks of my skin.

A willow's last shiver reflected in eyes
consumed by a darkly-struck soul full of lies
that waits for the earth and the sky to unite
horizons of chance in the fateless black night.
But slowly my shadow unburdens the ground
and flees from this prison, emotions unbound —
my only escape from chaotic unrest
is my own thudding heart inside of this chest
as time keeps on ticking away at the years,
a deep bell that tolls all my unspoken fears.
The winter plucks strings of a mad violin;
I'm losing myself in the cracks of my skin.

The crinoline demon of summer forewarns
a last glance of roses unfurling their thorns
to waken the sun sleeping deep in my breast,
a flicker of warmth that's forever repressed.
I grasp at the edges of forgotten dreams
but only get hold of the sound of my screams
as with each ragged breath I fight to survive
this haze of emotions. I cannot revive
the girl who keeps promising hope to the blind,
but never steps out from the dark of my mind.
The winter plucks strings of a mad violin;
I'm losing myself in the cracks of my skin.

windflower

orchid   windflower
molasses-draped sky

you drip lilac from my veins
and curl each warm petal
into the secret places
made by years
of wandering spring

windflower
fragrant pillow sky

the moon
spreads arms of honey
across pale skin
freckled with a thousand
trembling stars

a toe dipped in bathwater
a rippling eye

i hide in folds of twilight

i hide in folds of twilight
nestled between sky and sycamore tree

i like it here,

the wind drowns my thoughts
in threads of cold breath
until they can only shiver,
curled into small word bubbles
that slowly float away,
lost among the stars....

green

i want to know
all the mysteries of the world

tuck them away in denim
in exchange for secrets
given freely to the night

like drops of clear rain

when the trite murmur of
willows weeping
is too much to swallow

and the water on my face
can't shroud the sadness
of a moon
   round like child eyes

searching for light
in a forest of dark hands

i grasp for that silent beacon
as the earth cries my soul to sleep

singing:

"i am green
   nothing but limbs and branches

so reach, little one,
reach madly for the sun"

cadence

silence chews the ends
of my hair

a nervous schoolgirl
unfolding psalms
to the warm thighs of spring

*

I am an ancient lute

your calloused fingers
pluck my soul-chords

unraveling sighs
with each tone
pressed
upon a century of skin

*

our eyes meet
across
a thunder of stars

and i lose myself

there is no moan
deeper than the rain

dark-locked

sadness
twists around my ankles,
tripping me
with every turn
of the moon.

i want to be up there,

staring down
at the tiny specks
of life below,

    lost
       in a haze of stars
instead of this maze
of silence
that hooks into my eyes
and draws out rain.

i want the chaos of night —

a song among stormclouds,
resting in a palm of sky.

the storm that crashed our picnic

we ran under the magnolia tree
sipped our beer and waited

laughing about mother nature and her flawless timing

the rain went as quickly as it came
and we were no worse for the wear

a little damp   a little buzzed
a little more almost in love

I won't remember you

the moon and i
we lay our hearts bare
and i won't remember you

not when the night shivers
so profoundly
like winter's cold lips
have pierced the soul of you

i swallow down years of trouble
stripped to the barest bone
whiter than the eye that looked
on me with scorn

as you told me not to cry
hiking up my skirt
murmuring an ocean of lies
between my thighs
and i didn't know it yet
but the sun began to die that day

a thread hung down
tinged red

the shame
of staying lost in this maze
picking through each step
laid down in stone

the cracks and i alone
we won't remember you

a heart caged on canvas

o, to be acquainted with the moon

jewel-eyed child of night
who slicks hair silver

grin like sharkskin
glinting madly among the stars

*

it spreads like dawn

golden fingers
lazy in throats

churning
   dizzy
bright
amber
     ecstasy

across unsteady ground

*

fire weaves
into untamed spaces
claimed only by god

until this moment

when tongues snake
and we ache for the touch
of skin
shivering so neatly
under the great curve of night

*

he looks at me with
   my eyes

and we are one

night rhapsody

you play me
like good jazz

an electric shock of sounds
shivering inside
each and every vein
as night wanes
with the moon's
last tremolo

and the stars
pluck deep chords
of twilight

hot fingers tracing
along
curved edges of sky
and rain-soaked skin

i break the waves with you

surfacing
   like a storm
full of cloud gasps,

pools of moonlight
bursting
the tides of
unwanted mornings

we ride the dawn slowly

drawing each breath
onto our tongues
as the music fades
into the heat of day

and i wrap myself
in the silence
left by your song

antithesis

another day wasted on
another worthless story

the unraveling of pride
always creates more tangles
than rain

*

he looks at the mirror's
haggard face

"hello again, asshole"

the teakettle warbles shame

*

half-empty bottles
sing on the bedside table

   (pillows just aren't enough
to choke out the sun)

*

a fly buzzes overhead

settles on a
rocking bedpost

he fucks to feel whole

*

she whispers sex
in his ear

and he is swayed
by the subtle promise
of her hips

*

thunder rolls in

making love with
steam eddies above
empty streets

a lone streetlight
flickers in the dark

time drifts backwards on deep moon eyes

you slip your words under my feet
easily
like a windblown river lost among the reeds
and i need to feel you
growing like weeds around me

the sea breathes salt from the west

a thousand miles of reaching trees
biting the soft of my skin
like sin
like god in a cascade of glass
jigsawed across the moon
you hold so neatly in your palms

i grasp for air to wrap tight around my chest
and asphyxiate any last trace
of blue
shivering inside your eyes

but winter still draws sunbursts
on cold cheeks

as i wait in silence

a dove sleeping
among dishonest clocks

the strangeness of becoming

i was a pile of loose ends
a tapestry unravelled
by years of curling winds

the well-traveled flesh
of a wandering star

i don't know how you found me
lost in the corners
of mismatched lips

your fingers traced wonder
inside my eyes

and slowly put me together again

the thin skin of your palm
brushing away sadness
left in creases of moonlight

and i sighed without warning
unaccustomed to closed seams

a crescendo of green

she loves me with long leaves

veins part
the thin layer of night
between our lips

uncovering moonlight
from within the rough bark
of winter

the rise from acquiescence

i tiptoe
through deep earth,
the sharp call of rocks
bites into flesh

as i reach
through a symphony
of moss,
laying bare this heart

that scribed your name
onto its throat;

a promise

no longer satisfied
by the stillness of water.

it's late

    and i am weary of silence

(a hush of dawn
   breaks across closed eyes)
this song has spent
too long
hiding in the ache
of your shadow.

grasping for spring

too many nights have flown
since the wind sang in shades of promise
echoing against the quiet
flutter of my heart:

"voi, sempre voi."

my veins hold within them
a cold october sky
crying out for color, but

the wine of yesterday is bitter
in the fierce song of my throat.

these rough buds cannot withstand
the fury of leaves; the gold eye of autumn
pierces grey haze with scars
that no longer fade in the sun.

a flurry of winter, and you are gone.

Pearls

a flower reaches across summer
to nestle in her hair, warm lips pressed
against a cascade of dreams
tossed over sore shoulders,

weary from carrying shadows
into the deep stare of sun.

petals drip from closed eyes
as she makes her way towards dusk,
every pearl of sweat hiding poetry

slowly unfolding itself to the moon.

Equus Nocturne

she moves,

a blur of legs opening to the breath of birds
curling their wings around nests
of azure rust,

the dust of dry lips scraping away
at the gracelessness of day.

the wind sweeps warm
across a maze of wild eyes
searching the skies for silence
within a hollow mouth of rain.

hush, hush.

      a heart beats .. ..

darkness and light unraveling
among the steady whisper of grass.

no proof of love

bound by night's troth,

the moon moans
beyond cold glass

as i wait inside this
   shivering nest of bones

for the wind
to stop blowing your name
across my lips.

Out of Sync

trapped under a sea of rock
and i wash my sins inside your eyes

loneliness feels too much like home
that i cant run away from my own breathing,
tripping over heartbeats
with each flick of the second hand

and the glove just doesn't fit like it used to

when we were something worth mentioning,
when the sea was full of mermaids
and the earth refused to scour away
the skin of our soles with her sharp tongue

no,

yesterday was never going to catch up
to tomorrow, no matter how many dogs
chased their tails and how many
stars leapt onto the moon to feel her
coldness against their bellies,

the world still spins us on our heads
and the dawn still breaks our hearts
with the rising and falling of a chest
desperately clinging to the last drops of air
scattered like freckles over bridges
slowly sinking into the darkness of night

tomorrow just wasn't close enough to kiss
with the passion that we needed
to survive the distance between each breath

art song

we sleep like faeries among
fallen leaves, windblown
and wild,
crowns of snow
    glistening in our hair

dawn shares our bed

newness savored
in each splash of light
across the eyes of
cold november sky

*

our love is small

jewel-like and delicate on our lips
but deeper than song
a rising chorus
from the throats of birds

and we understand
    in our own quiet way

that the morning
recognizes beauty
in flowerless meadows

in a single blade of grass

disgrace and the night apostle

night slipped into my room with him,

crept across my bed
and plunged darkness
deep inside me

as the moon watched in silence —

one cold, derisive eye
bearing down on once-new flesh

now split like a grapefruit
across pink-tinged sheets.

*

it was like science:
    cold, calculated

a bold move for one so young
but what was there to lose?

slinking down that dark street
lined with teenage ghosts,
husks of skin and bone

stripped of all decency
before they even knew that
betrayal
wasn't always certain

until it was.

*

i could feel the wind
bleach my insides bitter,

exacting revenge
with trembling fingers as it

sliced away the last threads
that tied me to this
worn-out body,

abused from the start by
the moon's unwillingness to shriek

and a sun
that never managed to find me
    in the dark.

a tree draped in winter snow

sunset draws breath
with every scattering of dust
across the pale horizon

scratching night out of rough bark

hands of silence
and a whisper of moon —

    she smiles
and i don't know who i am
or what to be

*

calm settles
in the empty space between stars

and i blink at the sound
of birds flying overhead

so monumentally quiet

consummation

i digest you like a good book
or a glass of red wine

you seep into each pore
and rest there

content

until morning breathes
sonnets across our skin

tracing sunlight
between my freckles
and your sighs

as we rise like smoke
from the last tangles of sleep

shaking off night like raindrops
the moon held soft between our lips

tend

i reach
for the torn edge
of a star
just to feel its fire
burn my fingertips

i know the moon well

she dresses my wounds
with cool water

transient

we saw a ghost
last summer —
   do you remember?

long hazy tendrils of honey
oozing down the steps,

   gliding onto the living room couch.

it caught the sun,
throwing arcs of color
across the walls

   and we could only watch,
stunned.

it was hours before the ghost
(content against braided upholstery)
finally melted away,
   soft butter in the night.

we didn't sit on that couch for days,

preferring instead
the feel of naked wood
against our thighs,

   two moon-glazed shadows

and an empty space
where our ghost used to be.

the dark within

your eye spins 'round like a marble
always looking down
a sound, plucked from the socket
of a pale face

your eye, the moon

*

too long have i been waiting here for you
the night grows blacker, darker still
it eats me through and through

ten years have come and gone and i outgrew
that wicked shoe that drops upon
my dreams with eyes of you

*

it found me once
inside the skin i tried to hide from
pale as sin

the moon, your eye
the dark within

*

i bled with every winsome lie you told
my ragged heart cracked into two
your eyes, they always knew

the stars don't warm the moments spent alone
i count on fingers cold and blue
each vein descends from you

*

i planted you in shadow
where lilies won't grow

but the darkness creeps up
to haunt me even so

your eye, the moon

ice and stone

The spiteful cry of night I do intone,
a groan, a willow's sigh and I
do mark it as my own.

To moan from lips that crack like wasted bone
or stretch across the faceless black;
to me, this feels like home.

But no one knows the drone of whispers cruel
as I do, words of ice and stone,
the only words I've known.

They reach through skin sewn fast with scars and lies,
the thing I scratch when I'm alone,
I scratch down to the bone.

The darkness dines on hate I can't disown —
my weary eyes clamp shut once night has flown.

petals

we held hands
at baltimore harbor

cherry blossoms
sang wild in our hair
kissing their reflections
in still water

spring bloomed that day

it nestled
between our palms

moonstruck at midnight

night keeps tucking itself
around me, an old woolen blanket
biting at my skin. i try to shrug it off,
but it seems to wrap itself tighter and
tighter, dark threads weaving their way
into the patchwork of my soul.

*

this merry-go-round wont stop,

not even for a glass of milk
or a kiss goodnight.

the wheel keeps on turning,
and i find myself with my head
on the ground
more often than i'd like.

*

i scrape my sides against sand--
a jagged shore gnawing at an ocean full
of paper boats

and a hint of something just out of reach.

*

i'm back where i started,
hiding within a shadow's breath
of almost, but not quite.

the night air stings my nostrils —

it burns like home.

three sheets to the wind

you steady me
when the sun hits my eyes,

smears
the back of my throat with such brightness
that i stumble
over every hint of smile
that begs to smooth my rough edges —

five a.m.

i lurch into bed and wrap myself
in the warm cotton
of your lips,

the taste of yesterday's scotch
still on my tongue.

ghost

you whisper phantom fingers
over a horizon of crooked birds
fluttering in my chest

like the wind's sigh
burns edges of breath

and i wait for you each day

as one hundred hands of sunlight
burst the seams of
dark velvet winter
locked away in a petticoat
worn only by the ghosts
that remember to keep
their elbows off the table
during days of endless sleep

*

i waste precious moments
deconstructing the sound of dawn
as it preens outside my window
every morning

golden beak
pecking away at my skin
like a paperbark tree

exposing young flesh
to scabbed knees
and sidewalk chalk mysteries
worn
by the memory of rain

*

smoke curls in my nostrils
and i forget what it is like
to feel the sweat of loving you
as it blinks beyond the grasp
of my subconscious

forget the feel of your voice
wrapping songs around my sorrow
like the sea

kissing salt from my skin
and tasting the hurt
in every summer
that wakes me to the hollow cry
where you used to hide
all your secrets

before eternity
etched your name
on the palms of dusk

and you withered
like ash
in the fading blush of sun

pareidolia

we dance among brambles

you, with your cold eye
and i with my thorn

too far to speak

volumes clamp inside ears
unaccustomed to such
impetuous song

you sing so prettily suspended in black

*

i am a mess of flesh

sharp angles and tangles
of vulgar breaths
    a caged winter, releasing
ravens into the brutal night

feathers melt like snowflakes
on pale skin

and i wrap a ribbon around
the distance between us
to keep from falling backwards

into the sun

Mad Ocean

The tide chases me around
a playground of broken dolls —
crinoline dresses
damp with salt,
cracked glass eyes
rippling in the deep breast
of night.

The sting of summer crawls
into my pores
and I wait inside each oncoming wave
as we spin wildly
in the storm:

Rock the baby to sleep,
mad ocean,
feel my fingertips draw
a promise through white foam
as you swallow us
into your wide blue belly.

We drag our hearts
across the same rough sand,
each carrying a secret
below cold skin.

The stars draw out
every tiny breath
thrumming
beneath the surface:

ten fingers pressed
against my chest;

ten toes curled
inside the moon.

slumber

silence crept in slowly
on waves of rain

upon finding him
gone
gone

you filled with white haze

more exhausted
than the sea

inamorata

night glazed us with moonwater —
two bodies slick with sweat,
and between kisses
i captured stars on my tongue.
their warmth passed
from me to you
through trembling lips

until dawn blinked,
light glancing
over bent blades of grass
where we shed our skin
and sank into the earth
    (into each other)
to the quiet hum of rain.

a moment

your heart flutters
against my mouth

an ocean
of hummingbirds
on lips

slick with summer

the leaves turn their cheeks
from the sun
and the wind stops breathing

for the briefest moment

just to hear another beat
echoing
in the dark

plucked

she sits,
pretty red flower on cold pew.

warm hands grope
underneath sunday best
as church bells smack their lips
to the patter of prayer
and patent leather —

the warble of god in her throat.

The Remains of Yesterday

The road is littered with failed attempts,
a silence that disconnects the lights
to another scrap metal palace
lost among a century of plasticine empires.
it was our fault —
we tried growing flowers
by planting seeds of destruction in dead soil,
our own private armageddon
wrapping smoke-choked arms around
every baby that never knew what it felt like
to crawl on soft ground —
scabbed knees and a stale breeze
and the whole thing crumbles to dust
under the neon lights of a 24-hour truck stop,
blaring out prophesies through a thick beard of smog
that smothers any chance
we might have had for redemption.

The traffic doesn't rock me to sleep anymore —
the whys and lies all catch in my throat
as I try to swallow the terror that claws at me,
constantly hoping for another way out
of this plexiglass maze,
but the stars keep finding places to hide at night,
between cracked cement mysteries
and churches overgrown with blasphemy.
I tell myself that God still has a home

in the cobweb corners of dark alleys,
but I honestly can't be sure;
they don't teach us to recognize miracles
in public school anymore.

It's only when the sun comes out
that I wonder why I've started holding my breath
every time I pass this graveyard of a town —
giving up on lives locked behind rusty doors,
memories trapped under layers of dust and decay.
I'm not sure I know the answer —
it may be one of those secrets
hidden in spray paint hieroglyphics
or lost between the lines etched across my brow.
Maybe it's staring us right in the face,
but we don't know how to interpret the signs;
after all, they don't teach us to recognize miracles
in public school anymore.

The point I'm trying to make is that we can't stop the world
from crumbling around our feet,
and we can't see tomorrow from a crowded street,
but the rain still plays jazz on a heap of rubble,
and the wind still swirls by
with the remains of yesterday tucked inside her pocket,
so if we close our eyes to the chaos
and listen a little harder to the rain,
maybe,
just maybe,
we might find something worth saving.

infidélité

i sit beneath the hand of winter
    bitter as tonic water
remembering all the lies you held
between clenched lips
kissing with eyes open

always your gaze on the moon

inside the void

the wind and i, we play a sad duet
to shed the burning of our eyes
and fears we can't forget

as sun spills acid breaths from every pore
that shiver in my moonless veins
like you, when i was yours

but night falls swift upon a heart possessed
and curls its bones inside the void
you left within my breast

your fingers strip the wasted flesh of stars
and rest them gently on your tongue
each one strung mad with scars

the darkness coos and all my will is gone
a fool am i for loving you so long

Red

the street was lined with red

red lipstick
red shoes
red cars

red red red

redder than the faces of crying babies
or the harsh smack of a palm
across the face

i remember how it was

you would strut over
stroking every inch of your ego

denim snake full of poison
ready to jump on anything with tits

i always indulged your little quirks

the nuances that made you come
out at night to that red-lined street
and lay your seige over used flesh
just to feel the shiver of skin
clenched around you

you felt like more of a man then

but you never noticed
that as you left

drained and dangling

i laughed at the image of you
dragging your sorry tail
back to the 'burbs

back to the life
that fucked you harder
than you could ever fuck me

and not pay you a dime
for the trouble

bouquet

cool water swells inside me

a wide mouth
opening to a flock of roses
newly plucked
    from the gentle breast of spring

i sigh as morning yawns quiet
as a cat bending itself
across the pale curve of my lips

glass humming under
earth-encrusted fingers

walking in search of sleep

i undress my eyes to the moon

laying my heart bare
as the night speaks
in cold shivers,

silver teeth that bite the
flesh from my bones.

the stars crack under my feet
as i reach the end of the world,

falling off the edge
until your smile breaks across
the belly of morning

and i can rest.

sacrifice

the children are playing outside

i can hear their laughter, see
them blur by the window
as i continue on, nose in book

anatomy, physiology, stacked like
the leaning tower beside me

a kite flies across the sun and
the room darkens
i grumble and reach for the lamp

a book falls to the floor
the hard slap of another lost Sunday

dissonance

his eyes were blacker
than the tongue of night;

they moved across my face
like an itch,
    his wandering gaze
the color of pitch and just as deep.

a thousand spiders
danced tunelessly inside that void

and i could so easily lose myself
in the dissonance
        of a love less pretty,

black chords that were thicker
than the first breath of winter
on pinked cheeks.

my skin was pale
mirrored in his irises,
cold and bone-white

and in the dark
i wept with firebirds
for the color left fading
among the ashes.

The Mockingbird

perched on a bare branch
    the mockingbird
sings a song about summer
while snow falls thickly
upon him

a blanket of irony
reflected in the sinister eye
of the moon

i wrap warm arms around you
plant kisses along
the curve of your breast

desperately trying to ignore
the buzz of my cell phone

my wife's disappointed face

the mockingbird's taunting hum

chiaroscuro

my mind muddles you

half-remembered chords
trapped
within the blurred chorus
of my subconscious

whispering
    in and out
of focus

before fading like sun
into the slow hum
of night

your eyes are more than color

only the moon
can paint a hue so bold
that the stars become jealous
and plunge from the sky

alighting on young branches
with trembling legs

driven mad
by the swirling pools of summer

forever locked inside your eyes

So Young

A burlap moon reminded me of home:
the smell of summer stretching out its arms,
a carriage house of stars content to roam
upon the stalls and rooftops of our barn.

In swaying fields of wheat, above our heads
the willow trees revealed their naked limbs
to anyone who cared to leave their beds
and climb, as robins whispered feathered hymns.

We dipped our toes into the quiet lake
as rain began to fall in lazy drips,
your eyes held shades of dawn barely awake —
a kiss of rose-tinged sun upon our lips.

The memories have wilted on my tongue;
I can't believe that we were once so young.

Two eyes, two lungs, one heart

winter lent me her sleeves
and i wear them willingly

two crooked pines
to keep out the bitter cold
as i walk the long road between
your eyes and the moon

seams burst under my feet
and stars erupt
a warm ball of honey

pools of sweetness
drawing arms around
my chest

leaving me breathless

shadows cast
by a mouthful of ghosts
slowly murmur night into my palms

tired islands melting
like a cube of sugar
into the sea

quietus

it was cold

the wind
brought ice
from the east

and the leaves
let go
of their trees

as if they knew
you were gone

The Promise of Rain

the wide milk of your body entices me

I want to paint myself inside
each freckle and hide there

lost within pale, pale skin

*

wrap a ribbon around my sorrow
and make me young again

when the sun was a cat's eye
blinking against blue curtains

and the moon whispered lullabies

because no one else remembered
how to speak to a child
with such wild hair

*

you reach across murmuring oceans
and smooth away the scars
that settled there

time crawls with long fingers
over the small of my back

promising rain

Gloom

time rests on the shelf

he steals a moment from its dusty throne
and steps out into the cold

night buzzes on his tongue
as he waits for the sound of moonlight
to come crawling back
over swells of rough stone

and softly touch his soles

courage

morning
promises winter
etched permanently
in moon flesh

so cold

singing in the dark
amidst nothing
but sorrow

hope

for when the last light
has gone out

haiku 1

rain on rooftops:
tiny footsteps echo
above sleeping heads

Fragmented

the wind stills the velvet warbling
of my sorrow

weaving tiny fingers
inside memories left wilting
in the feathered breast of spring.

*

we fed on wild blueberries

our mouths stained midnight
as the sun burnt through
loose cotton dresses

unfolding naked emotions
to the warm tongue
of an endless summer.

*

draw me your dreams
and i will give you the moon
hung like a lantern
under glass-laid stars

tile by tile

uncovering deep groves
hidden
beneath an ocean of skin.

*

piece together the minutes
with bits of cloud
and wrap the sun around my lips
to keep the sobs from escaping

a freckled eye
staring out the window

pretending to remember
what it felt like to be loved
amidst an eternity of rain.

The unmistakable calm of trees

dawn braids cottontails into my hair

weaving small fingers
into velvet coils
with the unmistakable calm
of trees.

the wind twines me in its roots,
a whispered mockingbird
through the curl of new leaves,

kissing away my tears

as willows nod their heads
to the song
of a thousand sleeping moons.

Clench

I am rubbed marbles,

dry wails of
glass on glass
echoing against cold
concrete caves of skin.

It drives you mad.

Bells shrieking,
you place
one clawed murmur
under my chin,

begging me to
pry open my jaws,

sparing two dozen diamonds
a long slow death
into the night.

The Night Parade

i weep in whispers,
seeking the feel of green
between my fingers
and the last kiss of sun before
the night parade begins.

grabbing fistfuls of sky,
i claw at white manes
and swallow mouthfuls of cotton
to take the day deep
inside my belly;

but no matter how hard i try,
the stars continue to put on
their sequined caps
and time-step across tar-black curtains
for seven billion sleeping admirers,

while i sit alone in the dark,
desperately clinging to my insides,
counting held breaths
until morning.

Exodus

birds sense which way
the sun smiles,
carving a path in the sky
toward longer days;

but i only follow the wind,
for it carries my heart
within its palms.

I am the travelling moss

Wind wrinkles a mosaic eye
as Winter flares
within my orchard heart,
an apple lurking
on deep hammocks of bone.

The sun's coreopsis fingers
burrow inside a belly of rotted wood,
digging into moondark corners
for secrets I buried long ago
among pigtails and rust.

I am the travelling moss,

unraveling ragged breaths
like a child,
sighing onto unfamiliar trees
as their leaves drip
from the tired mouth of Fall.

Water and Stone

i wander
among water and stone
as the wind chants
past centuries of silence
tamed
in these old bones

quietly
burnishing my spirit

Between the Trees

i hide in plain sight

whispers weaving
brightly-colored scarves
that trip like stones
over the still waters
of your lips

i sigh in ripples

scattering ancient breaths
along the pastures
of your neck
as i drink from the wide
chalice of night

and breathe a slow moon
to the tune
of a thousand willows

held deep within your eyes

Lonely Mountain (with Gray Kanarek)

I am a lonely mountain,

jutting unbroken from the plain
to face a mirrored east,
your sun rising in my closing eyes
from where I have hidden it
beneath this aluminum shell
(and in you I find the strength
to anchor myself in stone);

night folds into day.
I'll sleep when the cock crows.

*

There's a hole in my chest:
twelve centimeters of empty space
quivering with hollow blood whispers,

(secret silences three hours stretched).

I lay very still,
(dark and wet like moonlight)
and breathe in twenty-four hundred miles,
ticking off the seven hundred thousand seconds
till you finally come home with my heart.

*

I've been scoured
by the years, swept again
and again by subtle pinpricks

until nothing is left
but the tattered sediment
of my bones.

An echo of shrieking quiet
burns my ears:
white sky and sand
draw out endless ripples
(aching fingers reach madly)

in search of you.

*

The wind howls
and I waver,

crumbling into grains of sand
with every moment mapped out
in this unbearable silence,
(dawn-blinded eyes grasp for darkness).

Clutching at ragged edges,
I stand very still,
emptiness bleeding out of
tear-soaked pores;

deafened by the telescopic thundering
of my stone-bound heart.

(Shh… can you hear it?)

The Art of Crying

Tears fall thickly down my face,
lines drawn between freckles
and that scar you gave me
when I was twelve and stupid
and still believed in God.

I know better now.

I know what it is like to feel the sun
scorch bones raw,
scraping away memories
that scab over
before being torn apart
by the glaring eye of day.

Then night falls

and I remember
what it is like to cry
purely,
without fear
of losing yourself in darkness,

when the moon
fills up your lungs so completely
there is no room for thought,
only ecstasy so deep
it leaves you breathless.

I long for that asphyxiation.

haiku 2

winter:
evergreen branches
heavy with first snow

White Feather

it was my fault, your leaving;
i wished you out the door.

the tulips we planted
wilted under our tongues,
spreading black seed through
vulnerable veins, carving doubt
into deep moonless
rivers in my mind.

it was more than i could bear.

The long road home

the sun dipped low,

bright arms reaching
around the first bend
on the long road home.

she cried
for that cold and
lonely highway,

but her tears
evaporated;

tiny breaths

that never
hit the ground.

My eyes unfurl this moonless night

My eyes unfurl this moonless night
like screams within a saffron heart,
transforming darkness into art
without a trace of morning light.

The brambles weep their thorny light
upon the reckless tongue of night
as oceans yawn inside my heart
to wake from sleep, my silent art.

The moon will hide a touch of art
within the sun's repressing light
until the smoke of swirling night
perfumes a heady winter's heart.

I feel the creases of my heart
and breathe in wind's inspired art;
the willow's fingers hush the light
as skirts of stars caress the night.

A fractured heart makes sorrow art
until the night gives way to light.

winter

the deepest breast of sun

withers

like eyes
within warm sand flesh
as the wind cries dirges to the sky,

memories winking
through rough moonlight.

years slip by,

a wild milk thistle
held in your mouth.

When you are far away

I see the wind in shades of rust,

dragging two thousand miles of sand and silence
into my bed as endless mountains of stars
unbutton their tiny jackets
to feel heat rise with the eastern sun.

the desert catches in my throat
and I am breathless,
a century of old bones trapped beneath my skin;

but then night reminds me that
the same moon hangs in your sky as mine,
and I remember how to breathe.

hospital

i feel your heart wriggle
under loose cotton
while you sleep fitfully
beneath antiseptic moon;
hair matted with sweat,
eyes darken below
sallow skin.

as night staggers on
i refuse to sleep,
watching you slowly drift away
to the squeak of rubber soles.

China Doll

My little china doll
blinks like a cracked mirror
throwing phantoms to the walls:
secrets painted on dark tile.

*

It wasn't always like this.

I remember when the trees broke out in a sweat,
leaves popping like hot oil over the lawn —
you danced with the kind of grace
that can only be taught by the moon.

I remember your smile, a sprig of mint,
and the way the shadows came near
but wouldn't dare touch any part of you.

Autumn took you that day,
twining dandelion arms into your hair,
making you her queen

and I lost you to the swirling madness
hidden behind night's mask.

Dreams were forgotten,
tucked away in whispered curtains of youth.

There were no more bedtime stories;

you marched among sad eyes,
trapped within the furious calm
of pink ribbons slowly unravelling
tomorrow's empty promises.

*

My little china doll
waves her frown like a white flag,
desperate for one more glass of milk,

one more kiss goodnight

before Winter swallows you whole;

searching for something,
anything

to sweep away the crumbs.

Sideways Insane

my fiction heart drives you
sideways insane
into the eyes of a paper train
riding backwards through summer

a deep sea of words
a sad story
ripped out of my chest
like cancer

i chug moon-dreams
the size of courage
swallowing down
the briny darkness of night

caressing the spaces
between stars
like an old friend
yesterday's newspaper

floating through times square
a secret dance of ink
ignored by everyone
but me

Soldier

I feel a harrowing in my bones
as the moon strikes a match behind
her eyes; the glittering flame
douses any memory of Spring.

my breath unfurls
against the cold glass of night,
reflecting the darkness within.

a star streaks across the sky;

catching it lightly underfoot,
I bask in feeble glow for a long moment
before crushing it to a fine powder.

I sweep the remains into the sea —

a battle-worn soldier,
face utterly unrecognizable
in the mirror.

Night Terrace

the rain is heavy tonight

moist pearls
punctuate rooftops
as the moon softly braids night
into your hair.

low clouds creep over damp grass

and we settle
deeper into ourselves,
whispering untold secrets to the wind.

together, we breathe a quiet ocean

comfortably crumbling under
the weight of a thousand histories
being unwritten by the stars.

haiku 3

evening shadows —
pearls of moonlight
upon still water

Train Ride

I sit, nose against window
and watch hills stroll by:
green breasts dotted with clover,
blurred by glass and exhaust.

I have been here for days,
pretzeled in threadbare seat —
an attempt to break the silence
that once fused you to my bones.

Submerged in whistle-blows
and passengers chattering like crickets
on a starless summer night,

I rifle through memories
packed firmly away in mental rucksacks,
continuing to shrink the distance
between here and tomorrow.

The train and I are one,
two bodies patched together
with tenuous strips of hope;

always running,
never quite able to unbind
our feet from the rails.

A whispered song of summer

A whispered song of summer kissed my eyes
as, maddeningly caught and thus repressed,
a captured flower thrummed within my breast
to feel the sun against her petaled thighs.

I breathed a tongue of stormy silken sighs
to catch a drop of rain upon my chest;
the flower raised her head, so neatly dressed,
and swallowed all the clouds' reviving cries.

Her crimson fingers pressed against the skies:
a secret longing for the moon confessed
in darkness, where she kept her dreams suppressed —
inside my heart, among the thorns she lies.

I only wish that I could be as wise
as wild roses when the summer dies.

sated

i bask in the pink
of a lilting sky,

jewel-sweet summer
held between my lips.

i tongue stars and
nibble the moon,

savoring each sip
of night:

a hummingbird,
heavy with nectar.

Rebirth

Below the gazing eye of Ra
the sands of time evoke the west,
a murmured secret's lotus palm
entombed within my weary breast.

Thy desert winds restore and calm
as to my lips Osiris brings
a scarab sent to roll the sun
across the sky on golden wings.

I see the sacred ibis come
to scribe his book upon the sky —
the painted moon entwines my soul
with feathers so that it may fly.

My tears anoint thy earthly scroll
to hush the flutter of my womb;
the Nile guides my spirit home
as night enrobes this silent tomb.

silence

i went to the bay,
sat a while,
hummed a tune
and ate a sandwich.

after some time
I stretched out on the sand
and fell asleep.

when i awoke
i met a mermaid.

she waved her
damp golden hair around
and laughed like the sun.
i tried to touch her
but every time i got close
she disappeared.

i closed my eyes,
took a deep breath
and screamed;
it echoed across
the ocean
until it reached europe,
stumbling over the berlin wall
before eventually coming
to rest in front of a
tiny old woman.
she squinted at the thing
with wonder
before picking it up
and tucking it away in her
apron pocket.

"this will be delicious in tonight's stew",
she said,
and continued to walk home.

back on the beach
i opened my eyes,
feeling the silence
of four thousand miles
shiver inside me.

it was so beautiful.

surrender

reaching across
sad mouths

i split the moon

unveiling
her sweet crumbs
to the first
breath of night.

i shake the tears
from my eyes

and step across years
buried like bones
in the earth

broken glass feet
treading the miles
between every drop

of rain.

Bohemian Love Poem

i weave my heart around
wheat fields and willow trees,
placing a bit of myself into
every blade of grass --

a reminder
that i have always been here.

the sun exhales calm;
warm stars fill my belly
like freshly baked bread

and i am sated
until the next breath of light
seeps over the horizon.

Greeting my insomnia with a beer

the rain sighs outside
as i watch sitcoms
in darkened room,
unable to sleep.

laughter echoes from
pre-recorded midnights
stretched thoughtlessly
across typewriter memories
scrawling black words.

i remember how it felt
lying next to you at night,
two huddled bodies,

a crackling fire.

i wrap my legs
in a woolen blanket
to fight off the cold
slowly seeping in —

the fabric bites at my skin.

The Place Where Grasses Grew

I walked to the place where grasses grew;
a field of flowers is no place for me.
My feet were bare, my skin was hot
and as I stopped to listen to the silence
that wept all around me that hazy summer day,
I remembered what winter felt like on my tongue.

My eyes roamed easily like a cat's tongue
as my pupils with the darkness grew
like the sun when she first raises her head to the day.
It never made much sense to me
how the beauty of sound overtakes this silence
wedged between my lips, sticky and hot.

The night bore down, blazing hot —
it lapped at me with its scorching tongue;
wild birds made their way in silence
as the echos of my mind grew
like weeds, forever surrounding me
with light, even on the darkest day.

I wish there was a time of day
when the sun wasn't quite so hot,
that the air would speak in chills to me,
spreading breezes along my tongue;
but as I walked, my sorrow grew,
for I would never understand her arid silence.

But can one truly know the sound of silence?
I looked into the face of one more day,
knowing that, as summer's eye grew
despite the night, the sun's terribly hot,
fierce and gleaming tongue
would continue to consume me.

I'm not sure what happened to me
on that road paved with silence.
It rested on my tongue
as the sun cut a path through the day
like a candle, straight and hot,
which in the darkness grew.

The wild tongue of night reminded me
of flowers which grew in silence;
But I forgot to listen, on that hot summer day.

The Gardner

he cut the black bushes

coarse hairs
fell to earth like ash,
moondark and quiet
against the breath
of night

a naked heap of limbs

torn and gathered
into small piles
for collection
in the morning

i watched, unmoving,
as the remaining leaves
trembled

their brothers and sisters
scattered like ant hills
to the wind

This Mad Chase

You vanished from my heart without a trace;
the moon undressed her sorrow to the skies:
I pluck the scars that mar my inner grace.

The night erased the sun upon your face
while memories unfurled their silent cries --
you vanished from my heart without a trace.

I wish to tuck myself inside that space
where willows weep for Spring inside your eyes.
I pluck the scars that mar my inner grace.

Tomorrow never cut the threads of lace
that bound my soul to your deceitful thighs,
you vanished from my heart without a trace.

I crave a moment's rest from this mad chase,
a freedom from the mouth that kissed in lies;
I pluck the scars that mar my inner grace.

I reach inside the pattern of this place
to find within myself a song that's wise.
You vanished from my heart without a trace,
I pluck the scars that mar my inner grace.

home

grains of sand transect the lines
between chaos and tranquil lucidity
as wind's wrinkled eye
winks at the moon.

the sky spits out a star;

it bobs on the ocean waves,
desperate to make its way home.

Chasing the Dragon

i wasted my dreams
on powdered lines and
self-deception,
neat little rows
of fucked up glory
that dragged my ass down
to cold linoleum;
half-naked limbs
wriggling
like a hooked fish
in the glamour of too-bright light,
each spider shock
dissecting my spine with
phosphorescent orgasms
soaked in sweat and denial;
eyes cast in ice,
lids stuck open,
drowning in toxic vapors
that make you shiver,
make you feel
so fucking good
you don't even care
that you are slowly
crumbling to dust.

buttercups

you caught cloud whispers
on your tongue

the day i gave myself to you
in a field of buttercups.

threaded in moonlight
we shivered,

slick with love and yesterday's rain.

inside your words

i slip inside your words,

nestled against the thrumming
of language as it courses
through your veins.

i breathe in sonnets,

tongue each phrase
like a new lover,
sighs blooming out of every
untamed noun

as the tender lilt of poetry
lulls my loneliness to sleep

for just a little while longer.

Square Blocks, Round Holes

The wind whispered a sonnet in my ear
the morning you left me for a milkman
with college degrees in Marketing
and Go Fuck Yourself.
I know I was never that smart —
my favorite game as a kid
was sticking square blocks into round holes,
and to this day I still play that same game,
sticking square blocks into round holes
and planting my foot all the way into my mouth
until it comes out my ass like some gnarled tree trunk
that no one loves because flowers smell better
and are easier to look at than my tear-streaked face
after a half a bottle of vodka
and twenty-eight years of self-deprecation.

Maybe it was my fault,
cracking the lines that hover over land mines
and scratching the eyes of lies and whys and hows
or maybe I just didn't try hard enough
to love you the way you were taught

by your old Irish granny with the silver tongue
and more wrinkles than a dead chihuahua
splattered on the side of Sunset Boulevard
like a tiny encapsulated horror movie that no one sees
because they don't give a shit about real beauty.
The truth of the matter is,
I wish I was smarter so I could understand
how I bent your mouth into a frown
and chased your laughter away
the way that you're supposed to chase after your own destiny,
marching to the tunes of John Phillip Sousa
and the thudding of your own heartbeat against the rear windows
of Yesterday and Never Again.

But I'm not smart,
not like a German patent clerk or your milkman,
so I won't try to disconnect the wires
that plug experience into memory,
buzzing their way across my spine —
tiny sparks shocking my eyes out of greener meadows
and into the arms of my own dissatisfaction
with the life I have been dealt,
shuffling hearts the way the moon and sun
trade places every night,
back and forth, back and forth.
Instead, I'll just keep on trying
to accomplish the impossible-
sticking square blocks into round holes
until I fit inside my skin
regardless of who is standing beside me,
while I listen to the wind
whisper Shakespeare in my ear;
because even if I don't understand it,
even if I couldn't possibly comprehend it,
I know that it's beautiful.

dinosaur bones

the doll-faced girls in white dresses
make old men leer
as they lick melted sweetness
off pale sticky fingers,
squinting into
summer's gaping mouth —

naked, exposed and blazing.

they dream of skinned knees
and faded jeans,
violent tongue kisses
and a deep throbbing moon,

all the while making sure
the bright clean of their dresses
stays bleached
as dinosaur bones in the sun.

unease

the wind howls a bright red coin

i can see it from my window
splashing watermelon seeds
against the sky.

walking the floorboards, again

i feel the shudder of trees
under my feet —
severed tendrils struggling to breathe
through layers of collapsing Spring.

too many nights
have passed since dry eyes

only damp earlobes sit here now,
wrapped up in a white coverlet
meant to shield us from the snow.

Cloudburst

i look into eyes
glazed like ceramic bowls,

    pale as the moon

and remember
how your clementine hands
    caressed away sorrow,

your handkerchief smile
collected my tears,
    hung around your throat

    like pearls.

now you are gone,
    and in this moment

i wish it had been me,

for i have
cried a cloudburst

    and you deserve the sea.

paper hearts, origami cranes

i broke my body for you, shredding bone
into matchsticks littering the floor
around your feet.

i braided veins into paper hearts
and curled myself around your eyelashes
just to absorb the scent of your tears.

i contorted every fragment of myself
into a shape i thought you might recognize
until there was nothing left but an empty husk

and nine hundred and ninety-nine origami cranes.

Where Nothing Speaks

you keep your lips clamped
tighter than the moon,
who never whispered any secrets to me,
only stared into my window
and watched as i suffered

blow upon blow;

words you can't take back
because
they have been permanently
etched onto skin.

you and the moon,
you're the same —
cold, unblinking eyes that see
everything
from impenetrable distance;

a bystander

hung in the sky like paper lanterns
or a lost balloon from the park that will
eventually
deflate and choke a swan.

i know you well,
your very presence turns the ground
black
around your feet;

i will hide in that darkness —
wait for the lilies to bloom.

open and close

"open and close,"
says the mouth with the london smile.

i hear growling in the trees
and the sea speaks to me with icy fingers
tingling down my spine and through my hair,
craving the scent of salt upon skin.

winter makes the days longer
and the wild hordes transcend world's end
like small children in a third world village,
all alone,
without so much as a rag doll.

sometimes the sky drowns out the sounds
of people buzzing like bees along sidewalk,
reaching for stars
but getting caught in the storm.

tingling moods strike my limbs and
make me fall,
tumbling to the ground like a broken anthill,
upturned and full of shame;

if only the queen could repair the damage,

but she is just a figurehead,
a black dot on the end of a pencil,
a period
at the end of an exceedingly
and excruciatingly long sentence.

poetry

fingertips etch lines
in the blank spaces of true inspiration,
ink streaming across
the metaphor of my subconscious.

words tumble-
black sparks and idle thoughts
caught in a net woven of swan feathers
and half-remembered dreams.

rain-soaked memories are written
across parchment skies
swollen with tears and calloused palms;

two hands kissing the air,
kissing each other.

Sunrise

You had gold dust in your fingers
and I buried my face in your hair
as sunrise crept with tiny feelers
across the curve of my spine.

Your lips fluttered over dark grasses
and south sea eyes,
and I rolled over, the flection of day
nestled between bare breasts.

I wrapped your mouth in honey
playing the delicate skin like violins
until you sighed,
catching my pearls on your tongue.

The king is in his counting house

If less is more and fewer is greater
than the sum
of all things worth subtracting,
I will pinch the skin below my eyes
and remember which numbers are prime.

(I have fewer gray hairs than Moses
and less time to count them than he did.)

The more mistakes we make,
the fewer risks we take,
inciting role reversals that
too few undertake.

If only less hate meant
fewer misunderstandings,
but we're too blind in the stomach
and hungry in the eyes
to know any better.

(I should leave fewer spaces
and drink less water
because this life has a tendency
to make too many promises,
less compromise,
and too few reminders to use up
all my refrigerator magnets.)

transposed in sky

your hollow bones
transect the lines
between my mind
and heart,

as feather-thoughts
alight designs,
transposed in sky
as art.

the night we shattered

we sit in silence,

a collage of broken words
scattered
across darkly tiled sky.

i hold you close
as stars tremor,

filling
a thimble moon
with wine and ink,

all your poetry
concealed
within satellite eyes.

Blank Pages

petals fall
from the roof of my mouth,
filling my eyes
with the scent of spring.

my dreams awaken grasses
from their long sleep
as tulips bloom into violins,
quietly plucking the stems
of misplaced youth.

clouds flutter their eyelashes
as tears fall upon
blank pages
filled with all the poetry
i felt so deeply inside my bones,

but never had the courage
to write down.

the girl who holds stars on her tongue

your eyes glint like cosmoid scales,
shaping the ebb and flow of time
with only boldness of thought.

we dance like clockwork mice
to flightless tunes of words
that have no meaning,
unless spoken by a girl with
a chestnut in her hair
and the desire to make things more complete.

it's not like the moon smiles
any brighter when we are alone,
but the spiny backbone of yesterday
flutters on ebon wings
into the cold recesses of night
and plucks out the stars with inky fingers,
swallowing them whole.

we weep our sorrows into loam,
from which come tiny green sparks
that slither out into the sweat of day,
only to dry up like fading memories in the sun;

but when the moon peels off her obsidian mask
to reveal your face and the world
turns on its head like a spun coin,
we are left wondering which way is up.

still the words hide their faces
in the chestnut hair of a girl
who holds stars on her tongue
and the desire to make things more complete,
until yesterdays become tomorrows
and sorrows grow like weeds
in the untended gardens of the mind,
penetrating every crack and crevice
of what was once perfect emptiness.

Searching Stumbling Upon Sad Eyes

I called to you from across the sea
but you were too far,
so I carved a hole in the sky
plunging a thousand deep ocean eyes
in search of any little piece of you.
I pressed my senses against every corner,
slicing through black bread and honey
when I heard someone weeping.
I looked up
and saw the Moon open her enormous jaws
to swallow the stars,
tears rolling down her cratered face.
I asked her why she was sad;
she said that she felt cold, and so very alone
suspended within night's profound agar.
I agreed,
and so we huddled together for warmth,
the blaze of a billion stars
under her tongue.

blackness

deep waves of your soul
swathe cold limbs like honeycomb
crushed
against too moist lips.

blackness tickles
where once
your mouth traveled,

lash by lash

along fault lines of dry eyes,
reaching inside warm folds
of surrounding skin;

almost perfect flesh
pressed into worn coat pockets,

quietly thumbing the holes.

Believing in the unbelievable

[a bird trilled at the moon.]

i like to believe in the unbelievable
so that when the darkness
finally pulls its velvet curtain down
           over my eyes
i will remember what it was like to fly.

   [i looked at him,
       and he at me
and in that moment,

       we were one.]

The climb

The staircase of life spirals
infinitely up toward heaven,
each step
an empty casket
under endlessly weary soles,
but they say the climb is worth it.

I'd rather drink my tea and wait.

star-crossed

under blanket of stars

hands touch
through hole in fence

fingertips press together
in whispered promise

a surge of warmth
on a cold winter night

paperbark tree

paperbark tree
stripped bare
by winter wind

burn burn the little prom queen

the unfortunate girls
risk too much
by risking too little,
oppressed by a parade of tyrant mice
climbing up their walls,
while she sits alone in a dim-lit room,
black velvet curtains over her eyes;
beautiful girl
can't see the writing on the wall.

i know her well,
cold tiara balanced on crooked mind,
sad jagged flower that scrapes
away at my skin, my sanity.
burn
burn
the little prom queen.

dust settles beneath
two layers of cotton and unkind thoughts,
bruised knees bent in masochistic prayer
over stone walls of small hearts;
another one of god's wayward children,
left naked on the steps of a broken-down palace
somewhere between heaven and kansas city.

i wonder if she dreams what i dream,
or if her unicorns have fangs that can pierce
the veil that separates us
by the blood of those lost to the
moon's midnight cravings;
all the poor lonely girls trapped in regolith,
shattered glass eyes peering
through cracks and craters,
no longer able to cry.

Broken Canvas

i tie you into knots

carefully twisted blossoms molding lips shut,
afraid a single uttered word
will tear our souls apart.

you waver before me
and i blink,

swallowing one last caress of your hand
before we creep
into a windowbox sky

curled pages of our hearts
fluttering
against the deep-set eyes of stars.

we listen,
clamped against the dawn

one broken canvas
and an infinity of tomorrows
blooming
between barely touching palms.

the crux of it all

thinking.
  dreaming.
spinning.

like molecules,
  i asphyxiate the knicknack realms of
    an undiscovered sky.

thinking
  without feeling;
or feeling too much,
numb with overstimulation.

blinking a bright eye,

i dance to the cobwebby operas
of a grapefruit moon,
dreaming of cold beaches and fancy old cars
    and bold, bold silence
        stitched up with shoelaces.

"why i am here?"
    i hear you call from under the thunder,
caressed by the wind and
  insatiable hunger.

i say,
"we are found
    in the meaning of trees
 and the swaying of knees.

        remember the days when we
would drive to the cliffs in your father's truck
to smoke and fuck?
    now we just sit and watch the stars."

that is the crux of it all:

      a life isn't measured by breath, or by time,
    but by how many stars we have watched
  explode into a thousand words,
and by how many of those words we have
 captured and pressed down in ink,
    or caught like a bone in our throats;
        one tiny warble of one immaculate star-

i wish i could reach them,
those shiny little faces.
   grab them by the shoulders,
kiss them with tongue.

i dream of the moon;

how her steel breast hangs heavy
in the sky
like a butcher's knife, carving
up the night with terrifying beauty.

The Start of Things

always the wheels turn over
onto themselves like ribbons,
wavy lines slashed across

the dirt-caked faces of my past.

the metronome rules
my stream of consciousness,
pulsing feverblisters of worry
and wishful thinking

reminding me
why i am constantly coming back
to the start of things.

i leave traces of my pain
on colored sidewalks;

wait for the rain to wash it all away.

treehouse

I feel the salt of summer sting my lips
as I sit above the clouds
in a treehouse filled with treasures
I have collected over the years

bottle caps and driftwood,
fish scales, moonstones
and conch shells

I lay them out on the floor
and touch each one in turn,
thinking of you.

pretend

i watch the hummingbirds
through slats of wooden fence,
one bright eye pressed against chipped paint
as they flutter like rainwater
in the stifling heat of summer.

the sun yawns to the chirping of crickets,
slowly tucking into the hills
as i suck on a blade of grass,
sweat clinging to my ribs, my lashes.

the moon and sun kiss
as they cross paths in the sky,
and i pretend that i am alone in a world
where there is no war or murder,
no angry stepfathers
or mothers who drink too much —

nothing but me, the moon,
and the hummingbirds.

sugar

Aching with the emptiness of an
overturned saucer,
I press my finger into your
sugar
just to feel the sweet crumbs
bite against my flesh.

Burden and Butterflies

I wade through the inky black,
obscure and illusive —
a rhapsody of
phosphorescent waves,
ebbing and flowing.

I wait for them to come:
the hapless brigade
of tiny tin toes
curling around every
alliteration, every rhyme.
Within a stormcloud of
burden and butterflies,
they appear
lucid and ever contracting.

They buzz inside me —
little beads of inspiration,
flitting around my mind.
Sometimes they are
too fast to catch,
but other times
they trudge along, and
I am able to encase them
in my delicate grasp.

You can see them inside
every teardrop,
rotating slowly in technicolor,
impervious to the chaos that
rains down upon my face.
I catch them on my tongue,
like snowflakes —
desperately etching them
onto my soul
before they melt away.

Phantasm

Wafting through the winter air,
a cold calamity rushes back,
filling my lungs with the acrid taste
of cigarette smoke and
an intense longing for the world
I lost to the bittersweet sounds of
Mozart's Requiem and copulation.

I wish for once
that I could just breathe —
staccato, cold and precise,
like a metronome of white tile,
icy against sandpaper roughness-
a stark hospital gown of regret.

My mind jumps like tiny mice,
squeaking and fighting
for the last bit of cheese.
Which one holds the poison?
Is it better to starve or to die in
delicious agony, knowing
you have beaten them all to
that melting sweetness
weighing in on your
tiny, infected taste buds?

And I too scamper about,
looking, searching for
the next bit of life to
rocket my eyes awake; like
the static that holds the folds of
sweater together in the dryer —
buzzing and popping
as you try with all your might
to tear the two halves apart.

I sleep alone,
and whisper to myself
that my friends are coming.

Soon,
soon there will be peace.

when we were young

we were young,
standing on the
backs of dinosaurs;
a golden bell hung low overhead
as the sky peeled back its
leathery throat
to the feel of rain.

As I Walk On

The sun curtsies,
slowly spreading her skirts below the horizon
as I travel across
this dark and lonesome land.

I choose my steps carefully,
slowly picking my way across deserts
and high
treacherous mountaintops,
silence slowly eroding my resolve.

When the rocks turn bitter
and too sharp to climb,
I break them apart with the last of my
good intentions,
jagged teeth gnawing at my soles
as I walk on.

I tread on war and murder,
on insecurity and deceit and intolerance,
those vile worms that invade our hearts and
blacken our souls with doubt.

I grind them down with every step
until no sharp edges remain,
until there is nothing left but dust
and one tiny pebble.

I pocket it before returning home.

Arcana

And the way my mind
shuffles the memories is diffusive —
the ants build their towers
and I play the fool.

Welcome to our game of death —
the stakes are high,
but when the golden snake
encircles the sinewy neck
of the hanged man,
he dreams in flames
of glowing amber midnight rain.

No two lovers could remark
upon the strength the devil
gives to the world.
No judgement find,
for all is lost inside
a star's bleeding heart.

I hide inside this swirling sphere —
the sun revolves for me and mine alone.
O jest me not,
that the wheel of fortune turns
its ever-fixéd gaze on those
who walk the shadows,
losing themselves in the
swift reaches of chaos and madness.

We dance in the light of the moon —
the high priestess of the inky black night
casts her judgement like
marble stones on a frozen pond.

And we bow down to the hierophant,
mocking the bones of his crooked spine
and straight-laced sensibilities,
redeeming our justice from
every passing chariot —
Lord, grant me temperance in
these vile and insuperable times!

The empress and hermit
walk hand in hand,
upside down but intertwined —
like a secret kiss,
stolen upon the ivied walls
of a foreign kingdom.

Upset the emperor and
the whole thing crashes down
in sheets and rows of neat little numbers —
painted faces two by two
in mindless duet —
cheek against cheek,
heart against heart.

Magician with your deck of cards,
you think you've rigged the game,
but you cannot simply wave your wand
and know which cup holds the poison.
Swing your sword and flip your coin,
but it will not save you
from the outstretched arms
of everlasting darkness.

O no, the secrets have been locked away
inside the deepest chasms of the mind —
pure and incomprehensible,
where none may divine them.

Pressing the stars of your eyes

against my palms,
I feel your slow heat thrumming
through silk and stone.

I capture sunset on my tongue,
rolling it around my mouth
like a crushed berry,
the taste of your honey still clinging
to my lips.

i constructed a heart

i constructed a   heart
   of

bits of paper
and string
and placed it inside
     my chest;

it rustles
   like the {sea}

within

   this
graceless
crosshatch of

bones.

The Walk Home

  He sits alone

      breathing quietly
in the light of the moon.

Plucking a star out of
       the sky,
  he puts it in his pocket —

it jangles against his keys
    on the walk home.

The First Moment

You coil tiny baby hands
around my little finger,
cheeks like pink sand beaches,
or an apple, newly picked.

I want to kiss your eyelids, feel
the paper-thin fragility of your skin —
delicate rose petals
pressed to my lips.

Your butterfly mouth
holds in its pout
all of my most secret dreams.

I breathe you in and
every fibre of my being
remembers you,
the beautiful creature whose life
was once entwined with mine.

I gather you up within the folds
of a cornflower moon,
and in that trembling moment
when your head rests
against my fluttering chest,

I know perfection.

connect

the sun falls into the ocean
like a bucket in a well
and i say, "why the hell does
it matter?" but you never
say anything and just smile.
the moon waves hello
and you wave back
and i was never that good
at communication but
when we walk it's like two
souls dancing on train tracks,

weaving through raindrops
and trying our damnedest
not to get wet or get
slammed in the face by a
two thousand ton sign from
God on wind-up wheels with
glaring lights that seem to
constantly scream, "we all
connect, if you would only
shut up for two seconds and
listen to the wind blowing
through your hair or feel
the grass crush under your
feet you would understand."
but i never did before, and
i guess i still haven't really
learned how to be at home in
this worn-out cage of bones.
you always did, though-
you listened to the stars
whispering in your tiny ears
and smiled through your tears
that crazy secret smile
that drove me mad because
i could never hear what you
heard, and i couldn't even begin
to know what you know but
that's what makes it so crazy
beautiful - the fact that i'm
a mess and you are magic
and despite all the bullshit
we still connect.

i wish i knew you

i wish i knew you —
to grasp the inner thoughts
of every neuron
firing wildly in your heart.

i'd calculate the exact angle
your lip turns up at the corners,
and if the number of freckles
on your nose is prime.

i wish i knew you —
to curl up inside every exhalation,
losing myself in the glorious
tempo of your breath.

artfully, i place the pieces of(your heart)

artfully, i place the pieces of(your heart)
against my chest, breathing(as clouds
or soft rain)within blinks of wind chime

(your eyes)like stars pressed against
the moon's palms(unravels my Winter
heart)in the deep newness of dawn

a mouth so small i could capture it
(lips and tongue and teeth)inside a
paper cup and drink you in completely

artfully, i place the pieces of(your heart)
against my chest, inhaling(as rune or
new cotton)your most lovely petals

Sparks

The ladder of good intentions
was never as easy to climb as it should have been,
stumbling over cracked steps,
planks of wood torn from the crab apple tree
that grew in the backyard of my mind,
while you caught cores in your throat
like tears, or a wish for something better.

At least, that's how I remember it.

We used to walk in the sun,
two birds with waxen wings,
as we talked about things like the moon and stars
and the makes of cars,
which was fastest in the race against time?

We didn't know it then,
but time always wins in the end.

And I know that sometimes my thoughts race too,
faster than sunlight, or gravity,
tiny word embers sparking around my head
without the grace of a fire,
and when that happens you sit back on your heels
and feel the feels that make you want to run,
but you know you only have a few bucks
and that shitty old truck
and could never outrace time —

so you're stuck.

And I'm glad for that —
though I hate to see you so sad,
crying tears through the years spent alone in bed,
with a teddy bear you call 'husband',
and a wish for something better.

We always pretended it wasn't happening,
but the words embedded like termites
in the skulls of our houses and the deep
wooded attics of our hearts;
you building flowers from cobwebs,

while I constructed a song out of
the sorrow between our barely touching fingers;
reaching out across the great divide
through a million miles of space
between a billion rotating atoms,
only to feel the distance increase exponentially
with each tick tock of the clock with
a sad face drawn in the spaces between our own individuality
and the need to compromise,
like a flag of surrender that no one waved because
we didn't think it was possible to give up any more
than we did yesterday.

The ladder of good intentions
was never as easy to climb as it should have been,
stumbling over cracked steps
as I shouldered the burden of my words like Moses;
hanging onto the broken pieces of remembered happiness
packed into life-sacks and buried in the backyard of my mind
while you caught my song in your throat,
swallowing your flowers like bitter tears
for a chance at something better.

At least, that's how I remember it.

Old Bones Crack with the Strain of Too Much Hope

[Lacrimosa dies illa,]

We braided our dreams
into golden idols,
fingers stained with
the hollow promise of salvation.

[qua resurget ex favilla]

poison seeped into our hearts,
embedded so deep that
we couldn't recognize
ourselves without pain.

[judicandus homo reus.]

The ground began
to crumble beneath us,
fiery tendrils reaching up
through cracks in our resolve.

[Huic ergo parce, Deus,]

We saw our redemption too late,
the path obscured
by the swirling ashes
of an everlasting darkness.

[pie Jesu Domine,]

Our souls fractured —
shards of self
lost among sightless eyes
and rotting flesh.

[dona eis requiem.]

Nothing remained but the embers
of a cruel and merciless fate,
weeping in the shadows
of our sins for all eternity.

[Amen.]

Pandora

i walk your underwater playgrounds
and dance to the tune of
a thousand violins,
bubbles popping with every stroke.

i dream of you in
technicolor lightning,
wasted by the moon's
everlasting sermon to the sea.

i ride the winds of chaos,

bleeding my desires into your
every breath;

like a moth to the light
i am drawn to you.

Snake

The wind howled a second time
and the trees whispered,
voices of the past echoing, echoing.
I heard them speak and knew their names —
I remembered everyone:
my mother, my sisters,
and I was a part of the deep swaying tree of life
that nurtured the sky with its breath.
The branches moved to the music of the wind
and I knew that too, once,
when I was young and beautiful;
but the moon laughs now,
and the time has come when dreams
are born not out of poison but of fear.

I lived in a time where men knew nothing;
I knew things, things I shouldn't,
but it demanded a price.
I stole them, I trained them, and from them
I took the things they loved most.
But I had to do it: it changed them.
I made them who they are, who they would become,
and I was right.
I was always right.
I did what had to be done.

I was their teacher.

Asphalt

[Say hello to the ones that came before —
    Remember them.
        Remember us.]

Remember them under the bleachers,
with their half-empty bottles of rum and
wicked, wicked grins.
Remember their forgeries —
eyes straying like a feral cat,
and one inky hand,
god-like in its omniscience.

[Bow down to the teeny tiny giants,
    ever consumed
        with their own gravity.]

Remember them drawn on playground walls
and bathroom stalls,
perverse and unkind.
Remember them in black and white,
chalky waves of conceit and belligerence —
the last remaining residue of life,
fading away on asphalt.

[Hopscotch me one more time,
    before our time is up,
        before it's time to die.]

Remember them.
Remember us.

clipped wings and silk screens

you look.
you stop.
you touch.

(is there something there under that
invisible cloak of conformation?)

you breathe in the vapors of retribution.

(hollow lungs gasping for release.)

you cry out your insipid fears of a
two-dimensional future.

(dry eyes pouring out
acidic puddles of emotion,
melting all over this facade.)

day turns to night.

the lights awaken,
one
by
one.
(the lamplighter knows his place.)

you walk around, thinking
serious thoughts, wearing
serious boots,
and never, ever
w o n d e r
about seriously reconsidering
all this seriousness.

(its all lies, anyway.)

a pigeonholed society
so cleverly shaded by
brushstrokes of painted pride.

(clipped wings and silk screens.)

you pretend not to see what's right in front of you.

(silly rabbit.)

you couldn't even if you tried.

A cobbled together emotional jigsaw

I walk a straight line to the corner of
East and Always, and as the road bows its
weary head under hard-soled intentions,
I wonder not where I am going,
but whether there is more grey
than blue in the sky today,
if the moon really is that Buffalo Nickel
I flung out my window when I was five years old,
and why you only love me when it rains.

wind against wing

i feel you in meadows —

acid-stained fingers of sun
cast shadows within folds
of blinding swelter;
and in parched, swooning hills,
morning eyes
rubbed raw with waking.

the gooseberries have shriveled,
plucked of their juice by your
torrid tongue
as lilies stretch their swan-necks
through cracks in dry earth,
desperate for the taste of rain;

but the birds do not abide
your fever
as they flit carelessly,
wind against wing.

Jupiter

I knew a girl once who spoke in tones of Jupiter
and walked the many-colored lines of the spaces
between shapes with too many sides to be able to
count by someone with a truck-stop education.

she spoke words like vanilla, or lighter fluid —
reaching out to me in big bold flames, but I
didn't know what the sound of tomorrow looked like
on the faded cobblestones of that dusty road leading
us all westward of salvation to a gas station
with too many memories inked on the walls of a
lock-up bathroom. (you never could see the moon
from under that acrid smell of futility.)

the quest for redemption was never meant
for the common man; we are too simple, too slow,
too stupid to know which way is up, or down,
or if there is even a difference (which there isn't
if you happen to be standing on your head...)

but sometimes, someone comes along and makes you
question everything you have come to know,
the letters you etched over and over in your clumsy
kindergarten hand become a foreign language and
you realize that you don't know anything and it
pisses you off, because daddy was always working,
and mama didn't know any better —

but when you look into the eyes of the girl who speaks
in tones of Jupiter, and walks the many-colored lines
of the spaces between shapes with too many sides to
be able to count by someone with a truck-stop education,
you know with absolute certainty and absolute clarity
that you might as well be standing on your head —
because redemption is impossibly far away
and Jupiter is even farther —
and you've never even seen the moon.

Little White Bonnet

Beating me over the head
with an umbrella
does not count as love, dear.
A kiss on the temple
from its steel rod
does not romantic make, dear.

You scorn me with your
little white bonnet —
preaching fidelity,
screeching fidelilty.

But why, dear, my sweet dear,
I humbly do entreat, dear,
as to how you could possibly
expect such things,
when you insist on
raging upon my person
with inanimate objects?

I promise you, it's raining not —
the sky is bright and clear, dear,
and you should have no fear, dear,
for I do dally not.

But perhaps, dear,
mayhaps, dear,
your umbrella could keep
the tears of pain
from draining down my face, dear.

For a single droplet from my eye
would make you think you've won.
And that, dear, my gentle dear,
can never be undone.

beautiful

Don't forget to breathe.

The grass tickles in-between our toes,
sprawled on the soft summer ground.
An ant marches slowly over the hole
in her faded denim jeans —
a tiny black dot on one pale
and scabby knee.
Beautiful.

We watch them tumble across the sky,
fluffy dragons and firetrucks,
the three little pigs, white as snow.
"I'll huff and I'll puff and
I'll blow you away,"
she said.
Turns out I'm not the only one.

Sun streams down through cracks in the sky —
everything is warmth and light,
almost iridescent.
Her ink-stained fingers play idly with a dandelion,
goldenrod against ballpoint blue.
I know it's a weed,
but not today, not today.

This is what love is —
not chocolates and candlelight,
or desperate, sloppy kisses,
but a tiny ladybug perched on
the ink-stained finger of a girl in
faded denim jeans,
lying in the grass beside me.

paper cranes

our shadows loomed
like paper cranes caught in the wind
while a kingfisher called,
echoing against laughter
and rippling waters.
you caught the sky in your irises,
dandelions in clenched fist
as tiny feet ran across damp grass
with the vitality of summer.
it was in that moment
we were young again,
your boldness washing over us
like sunlight
one unseasonably warm winter's day.

Zeno's Paradox

The door creaks on its hinges —
I roll a coil of hair between my fingers
and wait.
You stand there in silence
in that dreadful green raincoat
and I know what is coming —

My wallpaper skin peels back,
weathered and passé.
I hear your breath lilt and swoon
over the chime of the cuckoo-clock
and evening news.
Transfixed in the doorway,
carpet moulds to your footprint —
damp depressions exposing
every hesitation, every doubt.

I wait,
knowing all at once that you love me
and I love you,
and that it's irrelevant —
we can never cover the miles that
stretch out endlessly between us
in faded blue shag.

Alone

I'm alone, aching,
a hollow cage
where my heart used to live.
My bones feel brittle,
dry, like leaves,
or paper-
I can feel the edges begin to burn,
curling as they blacken
and turn to dust.

I'm wasted,
fading away with the land.
every bit of dirt,
every sprig of grass is
another piece of
my soul
ripped out of me,
buried under sheets of metal
and concrete.

I stand naked at
the center of the earth,
shivering and sweating,
the weight of it all
pushing me deeper and deeper
underground —
lines running parallel,
intersecting in places where
my spirit slowly decays
into mould.

I've lost myself among the roots
and whispers
of a time gone past,
becoming a part of the nothing
that precedes it.
This is my new beginning —
wholly pure and untouched
as we were meant to be,
and all alone because of it.

breakfast

You sing to me like morning fog,
releasing your thoughts in misty
furls over cups of lukewarm coffee.
We dance over kitchen tile, together

yet apart - you trying not to burn
the toast, while I make futile attempts
to complete just one crossword puzzle
without your help.

The microwave hums Chopin
in E-flat minor, and you smile at me
between sips of warm rain
as you push out your chair to leave.

I lean in and kiss your hair,
inhaling your music, a whiff of
aftershave, and a deep longing to stay.
And as the front door creates a divide

that feels like dissonance,
I sweep away the burnt edges and
empty spaces, the taste of your melody
still pretty on my lips.

Broken Dreams and Candle Wax

Tea lights dance over water
like sea birds,
silent and crowned in flame.
The path is illuminated —
each step reveals
tiny pinpricks of light,
beckoning, beckoning.

I walk the surface like glass,
fragile and icicle-cold,
knowing that every torment
swims below,
biting and snapping at my
sorrows.

I disentangle every
maze-like segment of bone
with unwavering precision,
unraveling the seams
that bind memory to skeleton.

Silence bares down,
reverberating
against broken dreams
and candle wax —
determination etched on every breath.

The lights flicker —
I douse them with a backwards glance.
I can still feel them thrumming
in this eclipsing darkness,
the singe still warm upon my
heart.

still waters

the phantoms of my past
    follow me like playfriends —
shadow puppets echoing against memory
and cold bathroom tile.

they braid themselves
into my hair,

    the smell of moonlight damped
below still waters.

scraped raw in fluorescent light,
their mirror grins
    coat my throat like a promise,

and as they paint my eyes with inky hands,
i rest my head —

lost
    in the steady murmur
of their song.

free dissociation

goodness wanting to be happy
like moon rain on a cold-washed night
the way your eyes penetrate my back like
spores dusting the sea a penny
i found in the ocean rusted like a
barnacle a treasure in my hand
daydreamers dance to the radiant
illustrations of time change dressings wild
without mending the icicle winding road
that you coffered without meditation
or mediation and when you look into
the sky of my irises the floods resume
liquifying every pore poison and heather
lavender lacing the strings of my heart like
a boot with the leather cracked and embossed
with horses and the wide mouth of the moon
swallows a rainbow whole dissolving
every color down down down like
a pink lemonade raindrop three times
more you sang and i talked and we
ran through the traffic like ducks
underwater flying soaring beautiful
agony and i wish the end wasn't so
damn sorry don't be left behind
the eyes only see in black and white
and i bleed in red.

Seams

Leaves crumbled, like
a broken mouth- hard,
cracked and rough as stone,
slowly eroding to dust.

The whirling wind picked up
the ashes of our past —
swirling, swirling.
It brought with it the cold temperance
of winter. The promise of warmth is all
but a deceitful dream
in this frozen wasteland.

We broke through lines and waves,
crashing into a thousand suns.
Submerged in the limitless depths,
we sink and careen madly —
caught by the constant rippling
of nature's diurnal clock,
ticking, ticking.

We tore apart at the seams,
exposed and quivering,
vainly attempting to
lash ourselves back together again —
but the air was too thick, too hot
for such desperate proximity.

So we waited, hollow
and alone,
hearts wreathed in flame.
But the cold was coming.
Yes, in time it would
come for us all.

Storm

You reach inside me —
razor sharp edges
cut the walls of my heart
with every glint
of your acid tongue.

I feel the cracks,
open and trembling,
unable to withstand
the bitter onslaught
of your anger.

But every time,
I reach inside and stitch myself
back together again —
convinced that the storm brewing
endlessly behind your eyes
has finally passed.

the ladder you built

i climbed the ladder you built for me
    out of sugarcoated lies

  and listened while
you remarked on how the varnish
     brought out amber flecks in my eyes,
         how the grain swirled like
     your heart
when i walked into the room.

  you told me
that the tree it used to be was
    taller than the moon,
with branches
       gasping
           for a taste of blue sky
   among red-throated birds.

and i believed you,
    the feel of wood under my palms

  like a promise.

  you urged me forward,
every step strewing
      pebbles and
         crumbs of my soul.

  i'm still not sure how it happened,
but when i reached the top of
    the ladder you built,

my heart   was nothing
   but the echo of a swallow;
     my voice,

     a trembling finger
  of the sea.

Hello There, Little One

hello there, little one.
i see you twinkling
so prettily up there.
i know you are big,
but to me you seem so small,
like a penny, or a pebble,
or a grain of sand.

you could fit so easily
in my hand —
hard and warm under
my calloused fingers.
i would hold you to my heart,
little light,
and feel your pulse against mine.

sometimes you hide
behind the clouds,
but i can still hear you,
humming your electric lullaby.
as i drift into dream,
your silver harmonies
echo softly in my veins.

i want to press you to my lips,
a gentle kiss goodnight.
you taste of lemon drops,
ice wine, burnt butter,
and smooth caramel,
melting slowly on my tongue.

i know your perfume,
that intoxicating mist —
i would recognize
you anywhere.
your swirling vapors
breathe life into me,
every night for the first time.

Bigger

I fell —
tumbling madly down
a dark rabbit hole of shame,
dictated to me in monotone
by a chain-smoking caterpillar
with an attitude problem.

The little boys laughed,
two by two,
each sound amplified
by the hollow crunch of
omniscient flowers underfoot.
I chewed my fate,
shrink-wrapped and frosted with deceit.

My dreams etched soundlessly
on the web-tongued creatures of old,
with golden horns and claws so sharp
as to tear you down
without ever descending past
the thickness of your porcelain skin.

Cocooned by a rainbow of
swirling, unending madness,
I went through that little house
and demolished what was left
of my broken spirit.

I wish I was bigger than that.

Big Fish Eat Little Fish

It ended suddenly —
running down
an endless hallway,
twisting lines,
like paperclip chains,
or daisies strung together
in the outfield.

You wore your crown like diamonds.

It's always dark inside the tunnel,
or astonishingly bright —
the path distorted,
green eyes blind.
Blue eyes mine.

Cross your eyes and dot your t's,
and if you please, we'll try again.

The waves crash over the sand,
each tiny crystal glittering
in the moonlight,
the feeling gritty underfoot.
I run, transected by the horizon,
the sand, the sky,
the unending darkness of the sea.

I see myself scattered among the fish,
like mirrors,
shards of self,
floating like shiny corpses
among the barracudas.

I remember you.

I remember
when your butterfly tongue
would take rest upon my mouth,
the thrumming of our hearts
like hummingbirds.

I ran from me.
I ran from us.

I remember me in pieces,
alone, crumbling to dust
in a forgotten corner
within the rust and shadows.

I ran in circles,
always ending back where I started,
over and over

until day was night
and you were gone.

I ran from me.
I ran from us.

Fondness makes the heart grow absent.

I wish I didn't know how this story ends —
from the way it began,
it almost seemed worth it.

i feel the chest of the world

heave under bicycle wheels —
   tattered ribbons and bits of lavender
wound into the spokes
             catch the breeze
like wild grasses undulating
against a darkening sky.

i ride the waves of cracked asphalt
   as snow begins to fall.
blinking against the cold, i ride to the places
        where hill and sky meet.

i ring my bell to tell them i am coming.

Made in the USA
Coppell, TX
19 September 2021